# VERDICT

by Agatha Christie

samuelfrench.co.uk

FOR PRODUCTION ENQUIRIES

UNITED KINGDOM AND WORLD
EXCLUDING NORTH AMERICA
plays@samuelfrench.co.uk
020 7255 4302/01

UNITED STATES AND CANADA
info@SamuelFrench.com
1-866-598-8449

Each title is subject to availability from Samuel French,
depending upon country of performance.

## MUSIC USE NOTE

Licensees are solely responsible for obtaining formal written permission from copyright owners to use copyrighted music in the performance of this play and are strongly cautioned to do so. If no such permission is obtained by the licensee, then the licensee must use only original music that the licensee owns and controls. Licensees are solely responsible and liable for all music clearances and shall indemnify the copyright owners of the play(s) and their licensing agent, Samuel French, against any costs, expenses, losses and liabilities arising from the use of music by licensees. Please contact the appropriate music licensing authority in your territory for the rights to any incidental music.

## IMPORTANT BILLING AND CREDIT REQUIREMENTS

If you have obtained performance rights to this title, please refer to your licensing agreement for important billing and credit requirements.

*VERDICT* was first presented by Peter Saunders at the Strand Theatre, London, on the May 22, 1958. The performance was directed by Charles Hickman, with sets by Joan Jefferson Farjeon. The cast was as follows:

| | |
|---|---|
| **LESTER COLE** | George Roubicek |
| **MRS. ROPER** | Gretchen Franklin |
| **LISA KOLETZKY** | Patricia Jessel |
| **PROFESSOR KARL HENDRYK** | Gerard Heinz |
| **DR. STONER** | Derek Oldham |
| **ANYA HENDRYK** | Viola Keats |
| **HELEN ROLLANDER** | Moira Redmond |
| **SIR WILLIAM ROLLANDER** | Norman Claridge |
| **DETECTIVE INSPECTOR OGDEN** | Michael Golden |
| **POLICE SERGEANT PEARCE** | Gerard Sim |

# CHARACTERS

LESTER COLE
MRS. ROPER
LISA KOLETZKY
PROFESSOR KARL HENDRYK
DR. STONER
ANYA HENDRYK
HELEN ROLLANDER
SIR WILLIAM ROLLANDER
DETECTIVE INSPECTOR OGDEN
POLICE SERGEANT PEARCE

# NOTES ON CASTING

SIR WILLIAM ROLLANDER may double with
DETECTIVE INSPECTOR OGDEN.
LESTER COLE may double with POLICE SERGEANT PEARCE.
Minimum number of performers: 8

# SETTING

The action of the Play passes in the living-room
of Professor Hendryk's flat in Bloomsbury.

# TIME

The present.

## ACT ONE
Scene One: An afternoon in early spring.
Scene Two: A fortnight later. Afternoon.

## ACT TWO
Scene One: Four days later. About midday.
Scene Two: Six hours later. Evening.
Scene Three: Two months later. Late afternoon.

# NOTES ON SENSITIVE TERMINOLOGY

Language used by the author in her stage directions and by her characters to describe mental and physical conditions and disabilities is of the period in which the play was first performed. We are confident that the author's intention was to be neutral within the stage directions – not to convey anything other than the facts of the characteristics relevant to a character's portrayal. The dialogue, however, is the embodiment of the character speaking and must express his or her intentions at that point in the play. This means that the author will have chosen terminology to be spoken with varying degrees of precision, sensitivity and, possibly, deliberate insensitivity according to the character and the circumstances in which he or she is speaking.

In our published version, therefore, we have applied the following logic:

• In stage directions, we have used terminology which is as neutral and factual as can be conceived, knowing that this will sometimes still fail.

• In dialogue, we have preserved the author's words as originally written.

We license this play on the basis that terms used in dialogue relevant to the physical and mental conditions of these characters may be changed in production to whichever best convey the author's intention for the audience. Sometimes this will be a neutral term, sometimes it will be a term which reflects the character's personality and/or the context in which they are speaking. Which of these applies is for directors and actors to interpret.

# ACT I

## Scene One

*(The living room of Professor Hendryk's flat in Bloomsbury. A late afternoon in early spring. During the course of the scene the light fades slowly for sunset. The flat is the upper floor of one of the old houses in Bloomsbury. It is a well proportioned room with comfortable, old-fashioned furniture. The main feature that strikes the eye is books; books everywhere, on shelves, lying on tables, on chairs, on the sofa and piled up in heaps on the floor. The walls are occupied by large built-in bookcases and a library ladder. Double doors lead to an entrance hall, down which is the front door, a door to Lisa's bedroom and a passage leading to the kitchen. Back inside the room there is a door leading to Anya's bedroom and a sash window leading to a small balcony. Karl's desk is filled with books as well as the telephone, blotter, calendar, etc. There is also a small portable work-table for Anya. Hanging on the wall by Anya's bedroom is a small set of shelves with more books and medicine in one corner. There is also a small cabinet with a record player on top. A sofa, armchair, three-tiered round table and a small console table complete the furniture. At night the room is lit by wall-brackets and table-lamps. LESTER is seen precariously balanced on the library ladder. He is a clumsy but likeable*

*young man of about twenty-four, shabbily
dressed with a tousled head of hair. There is a
pile of books on the top of the ladder. Now and
again,* **LESTER** *selects a book from the shelves,
pauses to read a passage and either adds it
to the pile or replaces it.* **MRS. ROPER** *is heard
off down the hall. She is a rather shifty and
unpleasant cleaning woman.)*

**MRS. ROPER.** *(Offstage.)* All right, Miss Koletzky, I'll see to it
before I go home.

*(**MRS. ROPER** enters the hall from the kitchen.
She walks with great stealth, entering the
room with her back against the wall. She is
carrying her outdoor clothes and a shopping
bag. She does not see **LESTER** who is engrossed
in a book. She creeps towards the desk where
there is a packet of cigarettes. She is just
about to pocket them when **LESTER** shuts his
book with a bang.* **MRS. ROPER,** *startled out of
her wits, spins round.)*

Oh, Mr. Cole – I didn't know you were still here.

*(**LESTER** goes to return the book and nearly
overbalances.)*

Do be careful. That thing's not safe, really it isn't.

*(She puts on her coat.)*

Come to pieces any minute, it might, and where would
you be then, I'd like to know?

**LESTER.** Where indeed?

**MRS. ROPER.** Only yesterday I read in the papers of a
gentleman as fell off a pair of steps in his library.
Thought nothing of it at the time – but later he was
took bad and they rushed him to hospital.

*(She puts her scarf around her neck.)*

Broken rib what had penetrated the lung. And the next
day –

*(She gives her scarf a final pull.)*

– he was dead.

**LESTER**. What jolly papers you read, Mrs. Roper.

*(Ignoring her, he becomes engrossed in a book.)*

**MRS. ROPER**. And the same will happen to you if you go stretching over like that.

*(She glances at the desk then back at* **LESTER** *again. Seeing that he is taking no notice she starts to sidle over, humming quietly to herself. She empties the cigarettes into her pocket then holds up the empty packet.)*

Oh, look! The professor's run out of cigarettes again.

*(A clock strikes five somewhere outside the window.)*

I'd better slip out and get him another twenty before they shut. Tell Miss Koletzky I won't be long fetching back that washing.

*(She picks up her bag, goes into the hall and calls.)*

Bye!

*(She exits through the front door.* **LESTER** *barely takes his nose out of the book.)*

**LESTER**. I'll tell her.

*(The kitchen door is heard to slam off.* **LESTER** *jumps, knocking the pile of books off the steps.* **LISA KOLETZKY** *enters. She is a tall, handsome woman of thirty-five, with a strong and rather enigmatic personality. She is carrying a hot-water bottle.)*

Sorry, Miss Koletzky, I'll pick 'em up.

*(He comes down the ladder and picks up the books.)*

**LISA**. It does not matter. A few more books here and there are of no consequence.

**LESTER**. You startled me, you see. How is Mrs. Hendryk?

**LISA**. The same as usual. She feels the cold. I have a fresh bottle here for her.

**LESTER**. Has she been ill for a very long time?

**LISA**. Five years.

**LESTER**. Will she ever get any better?

**LISA**. She has her bad and her good days.

**LESTER**. Oh, yes, but I mean *really* better.

> (**LISA** *shakes her head.*)

I say, that's tough going, isn't it?

**LISA**. As you say, it is "tough going."

**LESTER**. Can't the doctors do anything?

**LISA**. No. She has one of these diseases for which at present there is no known cure. Someday perhaps they will discover one. In the meantime... She can never get any better. Every month, every year, she gets a little weaker. She may go on like that for many, many years.

**LESTER**. Yes, that is tough. It's tough on him.

**LISA**. As you say, it is tough on him.

**LESTER**. He's awfully good to her, isn't he?

**LISA**. He cares for her very much.

**LESTER**. What was she like when she was young?

**LISA**. She was very pretty. Yes, a very pretty girl, fair-haired and blue-eyed and always laughing.

**LESTER**. You know, it gets me. I mean, time – what it does to you. How people change, I mean, it's hard to know what's real and what isn't – or if anything is real.

**LISA**. This bottle seems to be real.

> (**LISA** *exits to Anya's bedroom, leaving the door open.* **LESTER** *collects his satchel and puts some books into it.* **LISA** *can be heard talking to* **ANYA**, *but the words are indistinguishable.* **LISA** *re-enters.*)

**LESTER**. *(Guiltily.)* The professor said it would be all right to take anything I wanted.

**LISA**. Of course, if he said so.

> *(She glances at a book.)*

**LESTER**. He's rather wonderful, isn't he?

**LISA**. *(Absorbed.)* Hmm?

**LESTER**. The Prof, he's wonderful. We all think so, you know. Everybody's terrifically keen. The way he puts things. All the past seems to come alive. I mean, when he talks about it you see what everything means. He's pretty unusual, isn't he?

**LISA**. He has a very fine brain.

**LESTER**. Bit of luck for us that he had to leave his own country and came here. But it isn't only his brain, you know, it's something else.

> *(**LISA** selects a book of prose by Walter Savage Landor. She sits and reads.)*

**LISA**. I know what you mean.

**LESTER**. You just feel that he knows all about you. I mean, that he knows just how difficult everything is. Because you can't get away from it – life *is* difficult, isn't it?

> *(**LISA** is still reading.)*

**LISA**. I do not see why it should be so.

**LESTER**. *(Startled.)* I beg your pardon?

**LISA**. I don't see why you say – and so many people say – that life is difficult. I think life is very simple.

**LESTER**. Oh, come now – hardly simple.

**LISA**. But, yes. It has a pattern, the sharp edges, very easy to see.

**LESTER**. Well, *I* think it's just one unholy mess. Perhaps you're a kind of Christian Scientist.

**LISA**. *(Laughing.)* No, I'm not a Christian Scientist.

**LESTER**. But you really think life's easy and happy?

**LISA**. I did not say it was easy or happy. I said it was simple.

**LESTER**. I know you're awfully good – *(Embarrassed.)* I mean, the way you look after Mrs. Hendryk and everything.

**LISA**. I look after her because I want to do so, not because it is good.

**LESTER**. I mean, you could get quite a well-paid job if you tried.

**LISA**. Oh, yes, I could get a job quite easily. I am a trained physicist.

**LESTER**. *(Impressed.)* I'd no idea of that. But then, surely you ought to get a job, oughtn't you?

**LISA**. How do you mean – ought?

**LESTER**. Well, I mean it's rather a waste, isn't it, if you don't? Of your ability, I mean.

**LISA**. A waste of my training, perhaps, yes. But ability – I think what I am doing now I do well, and I like doing it.

**LESTER**. Yes, but...

> *(The front door is heard.* **KARL HENDRYK** *enters from the hall. He is a virile and good-looking man of forty-five. He is carrying a briefcase and a small bunch of spring flowers. He switches on the lights. He smiles at* **LISA** *and his face lights up with pleasure to see* **LESTER**.*)*

**KARL**. Hello, Lisa.

**LISA**. Hello, Karl.

**KARL**. Look – spring.

> *(He hands her the flowers.)*

**LISA**. How lovely.

> *(She puts the flowers on the table, takes* **KARL**'s *coat and hat and exits to the hall.)*

**KARL**. So you have come for more books? Good. Let me see what you are taking.

> *(They look over the books together.)*

Yes, Loshen is good – very sound. And the Verthmer. Salzen – I warn you – he is very unsound.

LESTER. Then, perhaps, sir, I'd better not...

KARL. No. No, take it. Read it. I warn you out of my own experience, but *you* must make your own judgments.

LESTER. Thank you, sir. I'll remember what you say.

(*He picks up a book from the table.*)

I brought the Loftus back. It is just as you said – he really makes one think.

(**KARL** *moves to the desk and takes some books from his briefcase.*)

KARL. Why not stay and have some supper with us?

LESTER. Thank you so much, sir, but I've got a date.

KARL. I see. Well, good-bye till Monday, then. Take care of the books.

(**LESTER** *flushes guiltily.*)

LESTER. Oh, I will, sir. I'm awfully sorry – more sorry than I can tell you – about losing that other one.

(**LISA** *re-enters from the hall.*)

KARL. Think no more about it. I have lost books myself in my time. It happens to all of us.

LESTER. You've been awfully good about it. Awfully good. Some people wouldn't have lent me any more books.

KARL. Tcha! That would have been foolish. Go on, my boy.

(**LESTER** *rather unwillingly exits through the hall and out the front door.* **KARL** *turns to* **LISA**.)

How is Anya?

LISA. She has been very depressed and fretful this afternoon, but she settled down for a little sleep. I hope she is asleep now.

KARL. I won't wake her if she is asleep. My poor darling, she needs all the sleep she can get.

**LISA**. I'll get some water for the flowers.

> *(She takes the flowers and exits down the hall to the kitchen. **LESTER** appears in the hall and comes back quickly into the room. He glances round to make sure he is alone with **KARL**.)*

**LESTER**. I've got to tell you, sir, I must. I – I didn't lose that book.

> *(**LISA** enters from the kitchen with the flowers in the vase. She quietly moves to the table and places them on it.)*

I – I sold it.

> *(**KARL** is not really surprised but kindly nods his head.)*

**KARL**. I see. You sold it.

**LESTER**. I never meant to tell you. I don't know why I have. But I just felt you'd got to know. I don't know what you'll think of me.

**KARL**. *(Thoughtfully.)* You sold it. For how much?

> *(**LESTER** is slightly pleased with himself.)*

**LESTER**. I got two pounds for it. Two pounds.

**KARL**. You wanted the money?

**LESTER**. Yes, I did. I wanted it badly.

**KARL**. What did you want the money for?

> *(**LESTER** gives **KARL** a rather shifty glance.)*

**LESTER**. Well, you see, my mother's been ill lately and...

> *(He breaks off.)*

No, I won't tell you any more lies. I wanted it – you see, there was a girl. I wanted to take her out, and...

> *(**KARL** suddenly smiles.)*

**KARL**. Ah! You wanted it to spend on a girl. I see. Good. Very good – very good, indeed.

**LESTER**. Good? But...

KARL. So natural. Oh, yes, it was very wrong of you to steal my book and to sell it and to lie to me about it. But if you have to do bad things I am glad that you do them for a good motive. And at your age there is no better motive than that – to go out with a girl and enjoy yourself. She is pretty, your girl?

LESTER. Well, naturally, I think so.

> *(He becomes suddenly confident.)*

Actually, she's pretty marvellous.

KARL. *(Laughing.)* And you had a good time on the two pounds?

LESTER. In a way. Well, I mean, I began by enjoying it awfully. But – but I did feel rather uncomfortable.

KARL. You felt uncomfortable – yes, that's interesting.

LESTER. Do believe me, sir, I am terribly sorry and ashamed, and it won't happen again. And I'll tell you this, too, I'm going to save up and buy that book back and bring it back to you.

KARL. *(Gravely.)* Then you shall do so if you can. Now, cheer up – that's all over and forgotten.

> *(***LESTER*** nods gratefully and exits through the hall and out the front door.)*

I'm glad he came and told me about it himself. I hoped he would, but of course I wasn't at all sure.

LISA. You knew, then, that he'd stolen it?

KARL. Of course I knew.

LISA. *(Puzzled.)* But you didn't let him know that you knew?

KARL. No.

LISA. Why?

KARL. Because, as I say, I hoped he would tell me about it himself.

> *(A pause.)*

LISA. Was it a valuable book?

KARL. Actually, it's quite irreplaceable.

**LISA.** Oh, Karl.

**KARL.** Poor devil – so pleased to have got two pounds for it. The dealer who bought it off him will probably have sold it for forty or fifty pounds by now.

**LISA.** So he won't be able to buy it back?

**KARL.** No.

**LISA.** *(Angrily.)* I don't understand you, Karl. It seems to me sometimes you go out of your way to let yourself be played upon – you allow yourself to have things stolen from you, to be deceived...

**KARL.** *(Amused.)* But, Lisa, I wasn't deceived.

**LISA.** Well, that makes it worse. Stealing is stealing. The way you go on positively encourages people to steal.

**KARL.** *(Thoughtfully.)* Does it? I wonder. I wonder.

**LISA.** How angry you make me.

**KARL.** I know. I always make you angry.

**LISA.** That miserable boy...

**KARL.** That miserable boy has the makings of a very fine scholar – a really fine scholar. That's rare, you know, Lisa. That's very rare. There are so many of these boys and girls, earnest, wanting to learn, but not the real thing. But Lester Cole is the real stuff of which scholars are made.

> (**LISA** *has calmed down. She puts her hand affectionately on* **KARL**'s. *He smiles ruefully.*)

You've no idea of the difference one Lester Cole makes to a weary professor's life.

**LISA.** I can understand that. There is so much mediocrity.

**KARL.** Mediocrity and worse.

> (*He gives* **LISA** *a cigarette and lights it.*)

I'm willing to spend time on the conscientious plodder, even if he isn't very bright, but the people who want to acquire learning as a form of intellectual snobbery, to try it on as you try on a piece of jewellery – who want just a smattering and only a smattering, and who ask for their food to be predigested, that I won't stand for. I turned one of them down today.

**LISA.** Who was that?

**KARL.** A very spoiled young girl. Naturally she's at liberty to attend classes and waste her time, but she wants private tuition – special lessons.

**LISA.** Is she prepared to pay for them?

**KARL.** That is her idea. Her father, I gather, has immense wealth and has always bought his daughter everything she wanted. Well, he won't buy her private tuition from me.

**LISA.** We could do with the money.

**KARL.** I know. I know, but it's not a question of money – it's the time, you see, Lisa. I really haven't got the time. There are two boys, Sydney Abrahamson – you know him – and another boy. A coal miner's son. They're both keen, desperately keen, and I think they've got the stuff in them. But they're handicapped by a bad superficial education. I've got to give them private time if they're to have a chance. And they're worth it, Lisa, they're worth it. Do you understand?

**LISA.** I understand that one cannot possibly change you, Karl. You stand by and smile when a student helps himself to a valuable book, you refuse a rich pupil in favour of a penniless one. I'm sure it is very noble, but nobility doesn't pay the baker and the butcher and the grocer.

**KARL.** But, surely, Lisa, we are really not so hard up.

**LISA.** No, we are not really so hard up, but we could always do with some more money. Just think what we could do with this room.

> (*The thumping of a stick is heard from Anya's bedroom.*)

Ah! Anya is awake.

**KARL** I'll go to her.

(**KARL** *exits to Anya's bedroom. The music of a barrel organ is heard off.* **LISA** *picks up a book of prose by Walter Savage Landor and reads.* **MRS. ROPER** *enters the hall from the front door carrying a large parcel of washing. She exits to the kitchen, deposits it then re-enters and comes into the room with her shopping.*)

**MRS. ROPER.** I got the washing. And I got a few more fags for the professor – he was right out again.

(*She takes a packet of cigarettes from her shopping bag and puts them on the desk.*)

Oh! Don't they carry on when they run out of fags? You should have heard Mr. Freemantle at my last place. Screamed blue murder he did if he hadn't got a fag. Always sarcastic to his wife, he was. They were incompatible – you know, he had a secretary. Saucy cat! When the divorce case came up, I could have told them a thing or two, from what I saw. I would have done, too, but for Mr. Roper. I thought it was only right, but he said, "No, Ivy, never spit against the wind."

(*The front door bell rings.*)

Shall I see who it is?

**LISA.** If you please, Mrs. Roper.

(**MRS. ROPER** *exits through the hall to the front door.*)

**DOCTOR.** (*Offstage.*) Good evening, Mrs. Roper.

(**MRS. ROPER** *re-enters.* **DOCTOR STONER** *follows her. He is a typical family doctor of the old school, aged about sixty. He is affectionately at home.*)

**MRS. ROPER.** It's the doctor.

---

* A license to produce *Verdict* does not include a performance license for any third-party or copyrighted music. Licensees should create an original composition or use music in the public domain. For further information, please see Music Use Note on page 3.

**DOCTOR.** Good evening, Lisa, my dear.

**LISA.** Hello, Doctor Stoner.

**MRS. ROPER.** Well, I must be off. Oh, Miss Koletzky, I'll bring in another quarter of tea in the morning, we're right out again. 'Bye!

> (**MRS. ROPER** *exits into the hall, closing the doors behind her.*)

**DOCTOR.** Well, Lisa, and how goes it?

> (**LISA** *marks her place in the book before closing it.*)

Has Karl been buying books again, or is it only my fancy that there are more than usual?

> (*He busies himself clearing the books from the sofa.*)

**LISA.** I have forbidden him to buy more, Doctor. Already there is practically nowhere to sit down.

**DOCTOR.** You are quite right to read him the riot act, Lisa, but you won't succeed. Karl would rather have a book for dinner than a piece of roast beef. How is Anya?

**LISA.** She has been very depressed and in bad spirits today. Yesterday she seemed a little better and more cheerful.

**DOCTOR.** Yes, yes, that's the way it goes. Is Karl with her, now?

**LISA.** Yes.

**DOCTOR.** He never fails her.

> (*The barrel organ music ceases.*)

You realise, my dear, don't you, that Karl is a very remarkable man? People feel it, you know, they're influenced by him.

**LISA.** He makes his effect, yes.

**DOCTOR.** (*Sharply.*) Now, what do you mean by that, young woman?

> (**LISA** *shows him the Walter Savage Landor she has been reading.*)

**LISA.** "There are no fields of amaranth this side of the grave."

> *(The **DOCTOR** takes the book from **LISA** and looks at the title.)*

**DOCTOR.** Hm. Walter Savage Landor. What's your exact meaning, Lisa, in quoting him?

**LISA.** Just that you know and I know that there are no fields of amaranth this side of the grave. But Karl doesn't know. For him the fields of amaranth are here and now, and that can be dangerous.

**DOCTOR.** Dangerous – to him?

**LISA.** Not only to him. Dangerous to others, to those who care for him, who depend on him. Men like Karl...

> *(She breaks off.)*

**DOCTOR.** Yes?

> *(Voices are heard off. **LISA** moves the work table and sets it ready for Anya. **KARL** enters pushing **ANYA HENDRYK** in a wheelchair. She is a woman of about thirty-eight, fretful and faded with a trace of former prettiness. Mostly she is querulous and whining but on occasion her manner shows she had at one time been a coquettish and pretty young girl.)*

**KARL.** I thought I heard your voice, Doctor.

**DOCTOR.** Good evening, Anya, you look very well this evening.

**ANYA.** I may look well, Doctor, but I don't feel it. How can I feel well cooped up here all day?

**DOCTOR.** *(Cheerfully.)* But you have that nice balcony outside your bedroom window. You can sit out there and get the air and the sunshine and see what's going on all around you.

**ANYA.** As if there's anything worth looking at going on round me. All these drab houses and all the drab people who live in them. Ah, when I think of our lovely little house and the garden and all our nice furniture – everything gone. It's too much, Doctor, it's too much to lose everything you have.

KARL. Come, Anya, you still have a fine upstanding husband.

(*LISA takes the flowers and puts them on the work-table.*)

ANYA. Not such an upstanding husband as he was is he?

(*She turns to* LISA *who laughs before exiting to the hall.*)

You stoop, Karl, and your hair is grey.

KARL. That is a pity, but you must put up with me as I am.

ANYA. (*Miserably.*) I feel worse every day, Doctor. My back aches and I've got a twitching in this left arm. I don't think the last medicine suits me.

DOCTOR. Then we must try something else.

ANYA. The drops are all right, the ones for my heart, but Lisa only gives me four at a time. She said that you said I mustn't take more. But I think I've got used to them and it would be better if I took six or eight.

DOCTOR. Lisa is carrying out my orders. That is why I have told her not to leave them near you in case you should take too many. They are dangerous, you know.

ANYA. It's just as well you don't leave them near me. I'm sure if you did, one day I should take the whole bottle and finish it all.

DOCTOR. No, no, my dear. You wouldn't do that.

ANYA. What good am I to anyone, just lying there, ill and a nuisance to everyone? Oh, I know they're kind enough, but they must feel me a terrible burden.

KARL. You are not a burden to me, Anya.

ANYA. That's what you say, but I must be.

KARL. No, you're not.

**ANYA.** I know I am. It's not as though I am gay and amusing like I used to be. I'm just an invalid now, fretful and cross with nothing amusing to say or do.

**KARL.** No, no, my dear.

**ANYA.** If I were only dead and out of the way, Karl could marry – a young handsome wife who would help him in his career.

**KARL.** You would be surprised if you knew how many men's careers have been ruined by marrying young handsome wives when they themselves are middle-aged.

**ANYA.** You know what I mean. I'm just a burden on you.

(**KARL** *shakes his head at* **ANYA,** *gently smiling.*)

**DOCTOR.** We'll try a tonic. A new tonic.

(*The* **DOCTOR** *writes a prescription on his pad.* **LISA** *enters from the kitchen carrying a tray of coffee. She puts it on the table and begins to pour.*)

**LISA.** Have you seen your flowers, Anya? Karl brought them for you.

**ANYA.** I don't want to be reminded of spring. Spring in this horrible city. You remember the woods and how we went and picked the little wild daffodils? Ah, life was so happy, then, so easy. We didn't know what was coming. Now, the world is hateful, horrible, all drab grey, and our friends are scattered, and most of them are dead, and we have to live in a foreign country.

(**LISA** *hands a cup of coffee to the* **DOCTOR.**)

**DOCTOR.** Thank you, Lisa.

**KARL.** There are worse things.

**ANYA.** I know you think I complain all the time, but – if I were well I should be brave and bear it all.

(**ANYA** *puts her hand out and* **KARL** *kisses it.* **LISA** *puts a cup of coffee on the work-table for* **ANYA.**)

**KARL.** I know, my dear, I know. You have a lot to bear.

**ANYA.** You don't know anything about it.

> *(The front door bell rings.* **LISA** *exits through the hall.)*

You're well and strong and so is Lisa. What have I ever done that this should happen to me?

> *(***KARL*** *takes her hand in his.)*

**KARL.** Dearest – dearest – I understand.

**LISA.** *(Offstage.)* Good afternoon.

**HELEN.** *(Offstage.)* Could I see Professor Hendryk, please?

**LISA.** *(Offstage.)* Would you come this way, please.

> *(***LISA*** *enters followed by* **HELEN ROLLANDER**. **HELEN** *is a beautiful girl of about twenty-three. Her manner is self-assured and charming.)*

Miss Rollander to see you, Karl.

> *(***HELEN*** *goes straight towards* **KARL**. **LISA** *watches her sharply as she pours more coffee.)*

**HELEN.** I do hope you don't mind my butting in like this. I got your private address from Lester Cole.

**KARL.** Of course I do not mind. May I introduce you to my wife – Miss Rollander.

**HELEN.** How do you do, Mrs. Hendryk?

> *(***LISA*** *gives* **KARL** *a cup of coffee.)*

**ANYA.** How do you do? I am, you see, an invalid. I cannot get up.

**HELEN.** Of course not. I'm so sorry. I hope you don't mind my coming, but I'm a pupil of your husband's. I wanted to consult him about something.

> *(***KARL*** *indicates the others in turn.)*

**KARL.** This is Miss Koletzky and Doctor Stoner.

> *(***HELEN*** *turns to* **LISA**.*)*

**HELEN.** How do you do?

*(She shakes hands with the* **DOCTOR.***)*

**HELEN.** How do you do?

**DOCTOR.** How do you do?

**HELEN.** So this is where you live. Books, books, and books.

> *(She moves to the sofa and sits.)*

**DOCTOR.** Yes, Miss Rollander, you are very fortunate in being able to sit down. I cleared that sofa only five minutes ago.

**HELEN.** Oh, I'm always lucky.

**KARL.** Would you like some coffee?

**HELEN.** No, thank you. Professor Hendryk, I wonder if I could speak to you for a moment alone?

> *(***LISA** *looks up sharply from her coffee at* **KARL.***)*

**KARL.** *(Coldly.)* I'm afraid our accommodation is rather limited. This is the only sitting-room.

**HELEN.** Oh, well, I expect you know what I'm going to say. You told me today that your time was so taken up that you couldn't accept any more private pupils. I've come to ask you to change your mind, to make an exception in my favour.

**KARL.** I'm very sorry, Miss Rollander, but my time is absolutely booked up.

> *(***HELEN** *speaks with great pace and assurance, almost gabbling.)*

**HELEN.** You can't put me off like that. I happen to know that after you refused me you agreed to take Sydney Abrahamson privately, so you see you *had* got time. You preferred him to me. Why?

**KARL.** If you want an honest answer...

**HELEN.** I do. I hate beating around the bush.

**KARL.** I think Sydney is more likely to profit than you are.

**HELEN.** Do you mean you think he's got a better brain than I have?

**KARL.** No, I would not say that, but he has, shall I say, a greater desire for learning.

**HELEN.** Oh, I see. You think I'm not serious?

> (**KARL** *does not answer.*)

But I *am* serious. The truth is you're prejudiced. You think that because I'm rich, because I've been a deb, and done all the silly things that debs do – you think I'm not in earnest.

> (**ANYA** *finds* **HELEN**'s *chatter is too much.*)

**ANYA.** (*Interrupting.*) Karl.

**HELEN.** But, believe me, I am.

**ANYA.** Oh, dear – I wonder – Karl...

**KARL.** Yes, my darling?

**ANYA.** My head – I don't feel terribly well.

> (**HELEN** *is put out by* **ANYA**'s *interruption, and takes some cigarettes and a lighter from her handbag.*)

I'm sorry – er – Miss Rollander, but if you'll excuse me I think I'll go back to my own room.

**HELEN.** (*bored.*) Of course, I quite understand.

> (**KARL** *pushes the chair towards the door to Anya's bedroom. The* **DOCTOR** *moves to the door, opens it then takes charge of the chair.*)

**ANYA.** My heart feels – very odd tonight. Doctor, don't you think you could...?

**DOCTOR.** Yes, yes, I think we can find something that will help you. Karl, will you bring my bag?

> (*He wheels* **ANYA** *off.* **KARL** *picks up the Doctor's bag and turns to* **HELEN**.)

**KARL.** Excuse me, please.

> (*He exits.*)

**HELEN.** Of course.

> (*There is quite a pause.*)

HELEN. Poor Mrs. Hendryk, has she been an invalid long?

> *(She lights her cigarette.)*

LISA. Five years.

HELEN. Five years! Poor man.

LISA. Poor man?

HELEN. I was thinking of him dancing attendance on her all the time. She likes him to dance attendance, doesn't she?

LISA. He's her husband.

HELEN. He's a very kind man, isn't he? But one can be too kind. Pity is weakening, don't you think? I'm afraid I'm not in the least kind. I never pity anybody. I can't help it, I'm made that way.

> **(LISA** *picks up the coffee cups taking them to the tray.)*

Do you live here, too?

LISA. I look after Mrs. Hendryk and the flat.

HELEN. Oh, you poor dear, how awful for you.

LISA. Not at all. I like it.

HELEN. *(Vaguely.)* Don't they have household helps or something who go around and do that sort of thing for invalids? I should have thought it would be much more fun for you to train for something and take a job.

LISA. There is no need for me to train. I am already a trained physicist.

HELEN. Oh, but then you could get a job quite easily.

LISA. I already have a job – here.

> **(KARL** *enters from Anya's bedroom and collects a bottle of medicine and a glass from the shelves by the door.* **LISA** *picks up the coffee tray and exits down the hall to the kitchen.)*

HELEN. Well, Professor Hendryk, can I come?

KARL. I'm afraid the answer is no.

*(He pours some water from a jug into the medicine glass.)*

**HELEN.** You don't understand. I want to come. I want to be taught. Oh, please, you can't refuse me.

*(She comes close to him placing a hand on his arm. **KARL** draws back a little. He smiles at her quite gently and kindly.)*

**KARL.** But I can refuse you, you know.

**HELEN.** But why, why? Daddy'll pay you heaps if you let me come. Double the ordinary fee. I know he will.

**KARL.** I'm sure your father would do anything you ask him, but it's not a question of money.

*(**LISA** enters from the kitchen.)*

Lisa, give Miss Rollander a glass of sherry, will you. I must go back to Anya.

*(He turns to go.)*

**HELEN.** Professor Hendryk!

**KARL.** My wife is having one of her bad days. I know you'll excuse me if I go back to her now.

*(**KARL** smiles very charmingly at **HELEN** then exits to Anya's bedroom. **LISA** takes a bottle of sherry from a bookcase cupboard. After a slight pause, **HELEN** makes a decision and collects her handbag and gloves from the sofa.)*

**HELEN.** No, thanks, I don't want any sherry. I'll be going now.

*(She turns to go, then pauses and looks back. The **DOCTOR** enters from Anya's bedroom.)*

I shall get my own way, you know. I always do.

*(**HELEN** sweeps through the hall and out the front door.)*

**LISA.** You will have a glass of sherry, Doctor?

DOCTOR. Thank you. That's a very determined young woman.

> (**LISA** *pours two glasses of sherry and hands one to the* **DOCTOR**.*)*

LISA. Yes. She has fallen in love with Karl, of course.

DOCTOR. I suppose that happens fairly often?

LISA. Oh, yes. I remember being frightfully in love myself with my professor of mathematics. He never even noticed me.

DOCTOR. But you were probably younger than that girl.

LISA. Yes, I was younger.

DOCTOR. You don't think that Karl may respond?

LISA. One never knows. I don't think so.

DOCTOR. He's used to it, you mean?

LISA. He's not used to it from quite that type of girl. Most of the students are rather an unattractive lot, but this girl has beauty and glamour and money – and she wants him very badly.

DOCTOR. So you are afraid.

LISA. No, I'm not afraid, not for Karl. I know what Karl is. I know what Anya means to him and always will. If I am afraid...

> (*She hesitates.*)

DOCTOR. Yes?

LISA. Oh, what does it matter?

> (*She takes refuge in her sherry.* **KARL** *enters from* **ANYA**'s *bedroom.*)

KARL. So my importunate young lady has gone.

DOCTOR. A very beautiful girl. Are many of your students like that, Karl?

KARL. Fortunately, no, or we should have more complications than we have already.

DOCTOR. You must be careful, my boy.

> (*He sets down his glass and picks up his bag.*)

KARL. *(Amused.)* Oh, I am careful. I have to be.

DOCTOR. And if you do give her private lessons, have Lisa there as chaperone. Good night, Lisa.

LISA. Good night, Doctor.

> *(The **DOCTOR** exits, closing the doors behind him. **LISA** hands **KARL** the glass of sherry. There is a pause.)*

I'd better go to Anya.

KARL. No. She said she wanted to be left to rest a little. *(Pause.)* I'm afraid it upset her, that girl coming.

LISA. Yes, I know.

KARL. It's the contrast between her life and – the other. And she says she gets jealous, too. Anya's always convinced I'm going to fall in love with one of my students.

LISA. Perhaps you will.

KARL. *(Sharply.)* Can *you* say that?

LISA. It might happen.

KARL. Never. And you know it.

> *(There is a rather strained pause. They both stare into their glasses.)*

Why do you stay with us?

> *(**LISA** does not answer.)*

Why do you stay with us?

LISA. You know perfectly why I stay.

KARL. I think it's wrong for you. I think perhaps you should go back.

LISA. Go back? Go back where?

KARL. There's nothing against you and never was. You could go back and take up your old post. They'd leap at the chance of having you.

LISA. Perhaps, but I don't want to go.

KARL. But perhaps you should go.

LISA. Should go? Should go? What do you mean?

KARL. This is no life for you.

**LISA.** It's the life I choose.

**KARL.** It's wrong for you. Go back. Go away. Have a life of your own.

**LISA.** I have a life of my own.

**KARL.** You know what I mean. Marry. Have children.

**LISA.** I do not think I shall marry.

**KARL.** Not if you stay here, but if you go away…

**LISA.** Do you want me to go? *(Pause.)* Answer me, do you want me to go?

**KARL.** No, I don't want you to go.

**LISA.** Then don't let's talk about it.

> *(She takes Karl's glass and puts it with her own on the bookcase shelf.)*

**KARL.** Do you remember the concert in the Kursaal that day? It was August and very hot. An immensely fat soprano sang the *Liebestod*. She did not sing it well, either. We were not impressed, either of us. You had a green coat and skirt and a funny little velvet hat. Odd, isn't it, how there are some things that one never forgets, that one never will forget? I don't know what happened the day before that, or what happened the day after it, but I remember that afternoon very well. The gold chairs and the platform, the orchestra wiping their foreheads and the fat soprano bowing and kissing her hand. And then they played the Rachmaninoff piano concerto. Do you remember, Lisa?

**LISA.** *(Calmly.)* Of course.

**KARL.** I can hear it now.

> *(He hums. The front door bell rings.)*

Now, who's that?

> *(**LISA** exits through the hall to the front door. **KARL** picks up a book and glances through it.)*

**ROLLANDER.** *(Offstage.)* Good evening. Is Professor Hendryk in?

**LISA.** *(Offstage.)* Yes. Will you come in, please?

(**SIR WILLIAM ROLLANDER** *enters from the hall. He is a tall, grey-haired man of forceful personality.* **LISA** *follows him on, closing the doors.*)

**ROLLANDER**. Professor Hendryk? My name is Rollander.

(*They shake hands.*)

**KARL**. How do you do? This is Miss Koletzky.

**ROLLANDER**. How do you do?

**LISA**. How do you do?

**ROLLANDER**. I have a daughter who studies under you, Professor Hendryk.

**KARL**. Yes, that is so.

**ROLLANDER**. She feels that the attending of lectures in a class is not sufficient for her. She would like you to give her extra private tuition.

**KARL**. I'm afraid that is not possible.

**ROLLANDER**. Yes, I know that she has already approached you on the matter and that you have refused. But I should like to reopen the subject if I may.

**KARL**. (*Calmly.*) Certainly, Sir William, but I do not think that you will alter my decision.

**ROLLANDER**. I should like to understand first your reasons for refusing. They are not quite clear to me.

**KARL**. They are quite simple. Please do sit down.

(*He indicates the sofa.* **ROLLANDER** *sits.*)

Your daughter is charming and intelligent, but she is not in my opinion the stuff of which true scholars are made.

**ROLLANDER**. Isn't that rather an arbitrary decision?

**KARL**. (*Smiling.*) I think you have the popular belief that learning is a thing that can be stuffed into people as you put stuffing into a goose. Perhaps it would be easier for you to understand if it was a question of music. If your daughter had a pretty and tuneful voice and you brought her to a singing teacher and wanted her trained for opera, a conscientious and honest teacher would tell you frankly that her voice was not suitable for opera. Would never be suitable with all the training in the world.

ROLLANDER. Well, you're the expert. I must, I suppose, bow to your ruling on that.

KARL. Do you, yourself, really believe that your daughter wants to take up an academic career?

ROLLANDER. No, quite frankly, I do *not* think so. But *she* thinks so, Professor Hendryk. Shall we put it as simply as this, that I want my daughter to have what she wants.

KARL. A common parental weakness.

ROLLANDER. As you say, a common parental weakness. My position, however, is more uncommon than that of some parents. I am, as you may or may not know, a rich man – to put it simply.

KARL. I am aware of that, Sir William. I read the newspapers. I think it was only a few days ago that I read the description of the exotically fitted luxury car which you were having specially built as a present for your daughter.

ROLLANDER. Oh, that! Probably seems to you foolish and ostentatious. The reasons behind it, let me tell you, are mainly business ones. Helen's not even particularly interested in the car. Her mind at the moment is set on serious subjects. That, I may say, is something of a change, for which I am thankful. She's run around for a couple of years now with a set of people whom I don't much care for. People without a thing in their heads except pleasure. Now she seems to want to go in for serious study and I am behind her one hundred percent.

KARL. I can quite understand your point of view, but...

ROLLANDER. I'll tell you a little more, Professor Hendryk. Helen is all that I have. Her mother died when she was seven years old. I loved my wife and I've never married again. All that I have left of her is Helen. I've always given Helen every single mortal thing she wanted.

KARL. That was natural, I'm sure, but has it been wise?

ROLLANDER. Probably not, but it's become a habit of life, now. And Helen's a fine girl, Professor Hendryk. I dare say she's made her mistakes, she's been foolish, but the only way you can learn about life is by experience. The Spanish have a proverb, "'Take what you want and pay for it,' says God." That's sound, Professor Hendryk, very sound.

KARL. The payment may be high.

ROLLANDER. Helen wants private tuition from you. I want to give it to her. I'm prepared to pay your price.

KARL. *(Coldly.)* It's not a question of price, Sir William. I'm not in the market for the highest fees I can get. I have a responsibility to my profession. My time and energy are limited. I have two good scholars, poor men, but they rate with me in priority above your daughter. You will forgive me for speaking frankly.

ROLLANDER. I appreciate your point of view, but I am not so insensitive as you may think. I quite realise it isn't just a question of money. But in my belief, Professor Hendryk – and I'm a business man – every man has his price.

KARL. You are entitled to your opinion.

ROLLANDER. Your wife is, I believe, suffering from disseminated sclerosis.

KARL. *(Surprised.)* That is quite true. But how – did you...?

ROLLANDER. *(Interrupting.)* When I approach a proposition I find out all about it beforehand. That disease, Professor Hendryk, is one about which very little is known. It responds to palliatives but there is no known cure, and although the subject of it may live for many years, complete recovery is unknown. That, I think, speaking in non-medical terms, is fairly correct?

KARL. Yes, that is correct.

ROLLANDER. But you may have heard or read of a sensational new treatment started in America, of which there are great hopes. I don't pretend to speak with any kind of medical knowledge or accuracy, but I believe that a new expensively produced antibiotic has been discovered which has an appreciable effect upon the course of the disease. It is at present unprocurable in England, but a small quantity of the drug – or whatever you call it – has been sent to this country and will be used on a few specially selected cases. I have influence in that direction, Professor Hendryk. The Franklin Institute, where this work is going on, will accept your wife as a patient if I exert my influence there.

KARL. *(Quietly.)* Bribery and corruption.

ROLLANDER. *(Unoffended.)* Oh, yes, just as you say. Bribery and corruption. Not personal bribery, it wouldn't work in your case. You would turn down any financial offer I made you. But can you afford to turn down a chance of your wife recovering her health?

> *(There is a pause. **KARL** stands for quite a while then turns.)*

KARL. You are quite right, Sir William. I will accept your daughter as a pupil. I will give her private tuition and as much care and attention as I would my best pupil. Does that satisfy you?

ROLLANDER. It will satisfy her. She is the kind of girl who doesn't take no for an answer.

> *(He holds his hand out to **KARL**.)*

Well, you have my word for it that when they are ready at the Franklin Institute, your wife will be accepted as a patient.

> *(They shake hands.)*

That will probably be in about two months' time. It only remains for me to hope the treatment will be as successful as these cases in the United States seem to have been, and that I may congratulate you in a year's time on your wife being restored to health and strength. Good night, Professor Hendryk.

(*He starts to go then stops and turns.*)

By the way my daughter is waiting in the car downstairs to hear the result of my embassy. Do you mind if she comes up for a moment or two? I know she'd like to thank you.

**KARL.** Certainly, Sir William.

(**ROLLANDER** *exits.* **LISA** *follows him off to the front door.* **KARL** *moves to the desk and leans heavily on it.*)

**ROLLANDER.** (*Offstage.*) Good night.

**LISA.** (*Offstage.*) Good night, Sir William.

(**LISA** *re-enters, leaving the doors open.*)

So the girl wins.

**KARL.** Do you think I should have refused?

**LISA.** No.

**KARL.** I have made Anya suffer so much already. For sticking to my principles I was turned out of the university at home. Anya has never really understood why. She never saw my point of view. It seemed to her that I behaved foolishly and quixotically. She suffered through it far more than I did. (*Pause.*) So now there is a chance of recovery and she must have it.

(*He sits at the desk.*)

**LISA.** What about those two students? Won't one of them have to go to the wall?

**KARL.** Of course not. I shall make the time. I can sit up late at night to do my own work.

**LISA.** You're not so young as you were, Karl. You're already overworking yourself.

**KARL.** Those two boys mustn't suffer.

**LISA.** If you have a breakdown, everybody will suffer.

**KARL**. Then I mustn't have a breakdown. It's fortunate that no principle is involved here.

**LISA**. Very fortunate –

(*She looks towards the door to Aya's bedroom.*)

– for Anya.

**KARL**. What do you mean by that, Lisa?

**LISA**. Nothing, really.

**KARL**. I don't understand. I'm a very simple man.

**LISA**. Yes. That's what's so frightening about you.

(*The thump of* **ANYA**'s *stick is heard off.*)

**KARL**. Anya is awake.

(*He moves towards the door to Anya's bedroom.*)

**LISA**. No, I'll go. Your new pupil will want to see you.

(*She goes towards the door to Anya's bedroom but* **KARL** *stops her.*)

**KARL**. You do believe that I have done right?

(**LISA** *pauses at the doorway.* **HELEN** *enters from the hall.*)

**LISA**. What is right? How do we ever know till we see the result?

(*She exits.*)

**HELEN**. The door was open so I came straight in. Is that all right?

(**KARL** *is rather far away, staring after* **LISA**.)

**KARL**. Of course.

**HELEN**. I do hope you're not angry. I dare say you feel I'm not much good as a scholar. But, you see, I've never had any proper training. Only a silly sort of fashionable education. But I will work hard, I will, really.

**KARL**. Good.

*(He comes back to earth, goes to the desk and makes some notes on a sheet of paper.)*

We will commence a serious life of study. I can lend you some books. You shall take them away and read them, then you will come at an hour that we fix and I shall ask you certain questions as to the conclusions you draw from them. You understand?

**HELEN**. Yes. May I take the books now? Daddy's waiting for me in the car.

**KARL**. Yes. That is a good idea. You'll need to buy these.

*(He gives her the list he has written.)*

Now, let me see.

*(He goes to one of the bookcases and picks out two large volumes, murmuring under his breath as he does so. **HELEN** watches **KARL** intently.)*

You must have Lecomte, yes, and possibly Wertfor. Do you read German?

**HELEN**. I know a little hotel German.

**KARL**. *(Sternly.)* You must study German. It is impossible to get anywhere without knowing French and German thoroughly. You should study German grammar and composition three days a week.

*(**HELEN** makes a slight grimace. He looks sharply at her.)*

The books are rather heavy, I'm afraid.

*(He hands her the two books and she nearly drops them.)*

**HELEN**. Ooh – I should say they are.

*(She opens one, glancing through it.)*

It looks rather difficult. You want me to read all of it?

**KARL**. I should like you to read it through with especial attention to chapter four and chapter eight.

**HELEN**. I see.

**KARL.** Shall we say next Wednesday afternoon at four o'clock?

**HELEN.** Here?

**KARL.** No. At my room in the university.

**HELEN.** *(Pleased.)* Oh, thank you, Professor Hendryk. I really am grateful. I am indeed, and I shall try very hard. Please don't be against me.

**KARL.** I'm not against you.

**HELEN.** Yes, you are. You feel you've been bullied into this by me and my father. But I'll do you credit. I will, really.

**KARL.** *(Smiling.)* Then that is understood. There is no more to be said.

**HELEN.** It's sweet of you. Very sweet of you. I am grateful.

> *(She gives **KARL** a sudden kiss on the cheek.)*

> *(Coyly.)* Wednesday. At four?

> *(**HELEN** exits through the hall and out the front door. **KARL** looks after her with some surprise. His hand goes to his cheek and he finds lipstick on it. He wipes his cheek with his handkerchief, smiles, then shakes his head a little doubtfully. He goes to the record player, puts on the record of the "Rachmaninoff Piano Concerto", then goes to the desk and sits. He starts to do a little work, but pauses to listen to the music. **LISA** enters from Anya's bedroom. **KARL** is unaware as she stands there for a moment, listening and watching him. She tries to retain composure but suddenly breaks down.)*

**LISA.** Don't. Don't. Take it off.

**KARL.** *(Startled.)* It's the Rachmaninoff, Lisa. You and I have always loved it.

**LISA.** I know. That's why I can't bear it just now. Take it off.

> *(**KARL** rises and stops the music.)*

**KARL.** You know, Lisa. You've always known.

**LISA**. Don't. We've never said anything.

**KARL**. But we've known, haven't we?

>   (*A pause.*)

**LISA**. Anya is asking for you.

**KARL**. Yes. Yes, of course. I'll go to her.

>   (*He exits to Anya's bedroom.* **LISA** *stares after him in despair.*)

**LISA**. Karl. Karl. Oh, Karl.

>   (*She collapses miserably, her head in her hands.*)

## Scene Two

*(A fortnight later. Afternoon. **ANYA** is in her wheelchair with her work-table next to her. She is knitting. **KARL** is seated at the desk making notes from various books. **MRS. ROPER** is dusting the bookcases. Her vacuum cleaner is next to her. **LISA** enters from her bedroom, comes into the room and picks up her handbag from the armchair. She is dressed ready for going out.)*

**ANYA.** *(Vexedly.)* I've dropped another stitch. Two stitches. Oh, dear!

*(**LISA** takes the knitting.)*

**LISA.** I'll pick them up for you.

**ANYA.** It's no good my trying to knit. Look at my hands. They won't keep still. It's all hopeless.

**MRS. ROPER.** Our life's a vale of tears, they do say. Did you see that piece in the paper this morning? Two little girls drowned in a canal. Lovely children, they were.

*(She picks up the vacuum cleaner.)*

By the way, Miss Koletzky, we're out of tea again.

*(She exits to Anya's bedroom. **LISA** has sorted out the knitting and returns it to **ANYA**.)*

**LISA.** There. That's all right now.

**ANYA.** Shall I ever get well again?

*(**MRS. ROPER** re-enters and collects her duster.)*

*(Wistfully.)* I want so much to get well.

**MRS. ROPER.** Course you will, dearie, of course you will. Never say die. My Joyce's eldest he has fits something shocking. Doctor says he'll grow out of it, but I don't know myself. I'll do the bedroom now, shall I? So that it'll be ready for you when the doctor comes.

**LISA.** If you please, Mrs. Roper.

(**MRS. ROPER** *exits to Anya's bedroom, leaving the door open.*)

**ANYA.** You'd better go, Lisa, you'll be late.

**LISA.** *(Hesitating.)* If you would like me to stay...

**ANYA.** No, of course I don't want you to stay. Your friends are only here for one day. Of course you must see them. It's bad enough to be a helpless invalid without feeling that you're spoiling everybody else's pleasure.

(**MRS. ROPER**, *off, interrupts the calm with the sound of the vacuum cleaner and by singing an old music hall song in a raucous voice.*\*)

**KARL.** Oh, please!

**LISA.** *(Calling.)* Mrs. Roper. Mrs. Roper.

(*The vacuum and the singing stop.*)

Do you mind? The Professor is trying to work.

(*She is rather amused at the incident and* **ANYA** *joins in.* **KARL** *starts filling his briefcase with papers and books.*)

**ANYA.** Do you remember our little Mitzi?

**LISA.** Ah, yes, Mitzi.

**ANYA.** Such a nice, willing little maid. Always laughing and such pretty manners. She made good pastry, too.

**LISA.** She did.

(**KARL** *rises and picks up his briefcase.*)

**KARL.** There now, I am all ready for my lecture.

**LISA.** I'll be back as soon as I can, Anya. Good-bye, Anya.

**ANYA.** Enjoy yourself.

**LISA.** Good-bye, Karl.

**KARL.** Good-bye, Lisa.

---

\* A license to produce *Verdict* does not include a performance license for any third-party or copyrighted music. Licensees should create an original composition or use music in the public domain. For further information, please see Music Use Note on page 3.

(**LISA** *exits through the hall and out the front door.*)

**KARL.** Some day, sweetheart, you will be well and strong.

**ANYA.** No, I shan't. You talk to me as though I were a child or an imbecile. I'm ill. I'm very ill and I get worse and worse. You all pretend to be so bright and cheerful about it. You don't know how irritating it is.

**KARL.** *(Gently.)* I am sorry. Yes, I can see it must be very irritating sometimes.

**ANYA.** And I irritate and weary you.

**KARL.** Of course you don't.

**ANYA.** Oh, yes, I do. You're so patient and so good, but really you must long for me to die and set you free.

**KARL.** Anya, Anya, don't say these things. You know they are not true.

**ANYA.** Nobody ever thinks of me. Nobody ever considers me. It was the same when you lost your Chair at the university. Why did you have to take the Schultzes in?

**KARL.** They were our friends, Anya.

**ANYA.** You never really liked Schultz or agreed with his views. When he got into trouble with the police we should have avoided them altogether. It was the only safe thing to do.

**KARL.** It was no fault of his wife and children, and they were left destitute. Somebody had to help them.

**ANYA.** It need not have been us.

**KARL.** But they were our *friends*, Anya. You can't desert your friends when they are in trouble.

**ANYA.** You can't, I know that. But you didn't think of me. The result of it was you were told to resign and we had to leave our home and our friends and come away to this cold, grey, horrible country.

**KARL.** Come now, Anya, it's not so bad.

**ANYA.** Not for you, I dare say. They've given you a post at the university in London and it's all the same to you, as long as you have books and your studies. But I'm ill.

KARL. I know, dearest.

ANYA. And I have no friends here. I lie alone day after day with no-one to speak to, nothing interesting to hear, no gossip. I knit and I drop the stitches.

KARL. There now...

ANYA. You don't understand. You don't understand anything. You can't really care for me, or you would understand.

KARL. Anya, Anya.

> *(He kneels beside her.)*

ANYA. You're selfish, really, selfish and hard. You don't care for anyone but yourself.

KARL. My poor Anya.

ANYA. It's all very well to say "poor Anya." Nobody really cares about me or thinks about me.

KARL. *(Gently.)* I think about you. I remember when I saw you first. In your little jacket all gaily embroidered in wool. We went for a picnic up the mountain. Narcissus were out. You took off your shoes and walked through the long grass. Do you remember? Such pretty little shoes and such pretty little feet.

ANYA. *(Smiling.)* I always had small feet.

KARL. The prettiest feet in the world. The prettiest girl.

> *(He gently strokes her hair.)*

ANYA. Now I'm faded and old and sick. No use to anybody.

KARL. To me you are the same Anya. Always the same.

> *(The front door bell rings. He rises.)*

That's Dr. Stoner, I expect.

> *(MRS. ROPER enters from Anya's bedroom.)*

MRS. ROPER. Shall I see who it is?

> *(MRS. ROPER exits through the hall to the front door. KARL goes to the desk, picks up a couple of pencils and puts them in his pocket. Voices are heard off. MRS. ROPER enters followed by*

HELEN. *She is carrying the two books which she borrowed.)*

MRS. ROPER. It's a young lady to see you, sir.

HELEN. I've brought some of your books back. I thought you might be wanting them.

> *(She stops on seeing ANYA and her face drops. MRS. ROPER exits to Anya's bedroom. KARL takes the books from HELEN.)*

KARL. Dearest, you remember Miss Rollander?

HELEN. How are you, Mrs. Hendryk? I do hope you are feeling better.

ANYA. I never feel better.

HELEN. I am sorry.

> *(The front door bell rings.)*

KARL. That'll be Dr. Stoner now.

> **(KARL** *exits through the hall to the front door.* **MRS. ROPER** *enters from Anya's bedroom carrying a wastepaper basket.)*

MRS. ROPER. I'll finish the bedroom later. I'd better slip out for the tea before he shuts.

KARL. *(Offstage.)* Hello, Doctor. Come in.

DOCTOR. *(Offstage.)* Well, Karl, it's a lovely day.

> *(KARL enters followed by the DOCTOR.)*

KARL. I'd like a word with you alone, Doctor.

> **(MRS. ROPER** *exits through the hall to the kitchen, leaving the door open.)*

DOCTOR. Yes, of course. Well, Anya, it's a lovely spring day.

ANYA. Is it?

> *(KARL turns to HELEN.)*

KARL. Will you excuse us a moment?

HELEN. Yes, of course.

DOCTOR. Good afternoon, Miss Rollander.

HELEN. Good afternoon, Doctor.

*(The **DOCTOR** exits to Anya's bedroom; **KARL** follows him off, closing the door behind him. **MRS. ROPER** enters from the kitchen carrying her coat and shopping bag.)*

**MRS. ROPER.** It's too hot for the time of the year – gets me in the joints it does when it's like that. So stiff I was this morning I could hardly get out of bed. I'll be right back with the tea, Mrs. Hendryk. Oh, and about the tea, I'll get half a pound, shall I?

**ANYA.** If you like, if you like.

**MRS. ROPER.** Ta-ta, so long.

*(She exits through the hall and out the front door.)*

**ANYA.** It is *she* who drinks the tea. She *always* says we need more tea, but we hardly use *any*. We drink coffee.

**HELEN.** I suppose these women always pinch things, don't they?

**ANYA.** And they think we are foreigners and we shall not know.

*(There is a pause. **ANYA** knits.)*

I'm afraid it is very dull for you, Miss Rollander, with only me to talk to. Invalids are not very amusing company.

**HELEN.** I really only came to bring back those books.

**ANYA.** Karl has too many books. Look at this room – look at the books everywhere. Students come and borrow the books and read them and leave them about, and then take them away and lose them. It is maddening – quite maddening.

**HELEN.** Can't be much fun for you.

**ANYA.** I wish I were dead.

*(**HELEN** turns sharply to look at **ANYA**.)*

**HELEN.** Oh, you mustn't say that.

**ANYA.** But it's true. I'm a nuisance and a bore to everybody. To my cousin, Lisa, and to my husband. Do you think it is nice to know one is a burden on people?

**HELEN.** Do you?

**ANYA.** I'd be better dead, much better dead. Sometimes I think I will end it all. It will be quite easy. Just a little overdose of my heart medicine and then everybody will be happy and free and I'd be at peace. Why should I go on suffering?

(**HELEN** *is bored and unsympathetic.*)

**HELEN.** Must be awful for you.

**ANYA.** You don't know, you can't possibly understand. You're young and good-looking and rich and have everything you want. And here am I, miserable, helpless, always suffering, and nobody cares. Nobody really cares.

(*The* **DOCTOR** *enters from Anya's bedroom followed by* **KARL.**)

**DOCTOR.** Well, Anya, Karl tells me you're going into the clinic in about two weeks' time.

**ANYA.** It won't do any good. I'm sure of it.

**DOCTOR.** Come, come, you mustn't say that. I was reading a most interesting article in *The Lancet* the other day which dealt with the matter. Only an outline, but it was interesting. Of course we're very cautious in this country about the prospect of this new treatment. Afraid to commit ourselves. Our American cousins rush ahead, but there certainly seems to be a good chance of success with it.

**ANYA.** I don't really believe in it, it won't do any good.

**DOCTOR.** Now, Anya, don't be a little misery.

(*He pushes the wheelchair towards Anya's bedroom.* **KARL** *holds the door open.*)

We'll have your weekly overhaul now and I'll see whether you're doing me credit as a patient or not.

**ANYA**. I can't knit any more, my hands shake so, I drop the stitches.

**KARL**. There's nothing in that, is there, Doctor?

**DOCTOR**. No, no, nothing at all.

> (*The* **DOCTOR** *exits with* **ANYA**. **KARL** *closes the door. He ignores* **HELEN** *and collects his briefcase.*)

**KARL**. I'm afraid I have to go out, I have a lecture at half past four.

**HELEN**. Are you angry with me for coming?

**KARL**. (*Formally.*) Of course not. It is very kind of you to return the books.

**HELEN**. You are angry with me. You've been so brusque – so abrupt, lately. What have I done to make you angry? You were really cross yesterday.

**KARL**. Of course I was cross. You say that you want to learn, that you want to study and take your diploma, and then you do not work.

**HELEN**. Well, I've been rather busy lately – there's been a lot on...

**KARL**. You're not stupid, you've got plenty of intelligence and brains, but you don't take any trouble. How are you getting on with your German lessons?

**HELEN**. (*Off-handedly.*) I haven't arranged about them yet.

**KARL**. But you must, you must. It's essential that you should be able to read German. The books I give you to read, you do not read properly. I ask you questions and your answers are superficial. You have not thought or studied or reflected. You must *work*, Helen, you must *work*.

**HELEN**. It's such a bore, working.

**KARL**. But you were eager to study, to take your diploma.

**HELEN**. The diploma can go to hell for all I care.

**KARL**. (*Astonished.*) Then I don't understand. You force me to teach you, you made your father come to me.

**HELEN**. I wanted to see you, to be near you. Are you quite blind, Karl? I'm in love with you.

**KARL**. *(Amazed.)* What? But, my dear child...

**HELEN**. Don't you like me even a little bit?

**KARL**. You're a very desirable young woman, but you must forget this nonsense.

**HELEN**. It's not nonsense, I tell you I love you. Why can't we be simple and natural about it all? I want you and you want me. You know you do – you're the kind of man I want to marry. Well, why not? Your wife's no good to you.

**KARL**. How little you understand. You talk like a child. I love my wife.

**HELEN**. Oh, I know. You're a terribly kind person. You look after her and bring her cups of Benger's and all that, no doubt. But that isn't love.

**KARL**. *(Astounded.)* Isn't it? I think it is.

**HELEN**. Of course you must see that she's properly looked after, but it needn't interfere with your life as a man. If we have an affair together your wife needn't know about it.

**KARL**. *(Firmly.)* My dear child, we're not going to have an affair.

**HELEN**. I had no idea you were so straight-laced.

> *(She is struck by an idea.)*

I'm not a virgin, you know, if that's what's worrying you. I've had lots of experience.

**KARL**. Helen, don't delude yourself. I am not in love with you.

**HELEN**. You may go on saying that till you're blue in the face, but I don't believe you.

**KARL**. Because you don't want to believe me. But it is true. I love my wife. She is dearer to me than anyone in the world.

**HELEN**. *(Bewildered.)* Why? Why? I mean, what can she possibly give you? I could give you everything. Money for research or for whatever you wanted.

**KARL**. But you would still not be Anya. Listen...

**HELEN**. I dare say she was pretty and attractive once, but she's not like that now.

**KARL**. She is. We don't change. There is the same Anya there still. Life does things to us. Ill health, disappointment, exile, all these things form a crust covering over the real self. But the real self is still there.

**HELEN**. *(Impatiently.)* I think you're talking nonsense. If it were a real marriage – but it isn't. It can't be, in the circumstances.

**KARL**. It is a real marriage.

**HELEN**. Oh, you're impossible!

**KARL**. You see, you are only a child, you don't understand.

**HELEN**. *(Angrily.)* You are the child, wrapped in a cloud of sentimentality and pretence. You even humbug yourself. If you had courage – now, I've got courage and I'm a realist. I'm not afraid to look at things and see them as they are.

**KARL**. You are a child that hasn't grown up.

**HELEN**. *(Exasperated.)* Oh!

> *(The* **DOCTOR** *pushes* **ANYA** *in from the bedroom.)*

**DOCTOR**. *(Cheerfully.)* All very satisfactory.

**ANYA**. That's what he says. All doctors are liars.

> *(***KARL** *collects his briefcase.)*

**DOCTOR**. Well, I must be off. I have a consultation at half past four. Good-bye, Anya. Good afternoon, Miss Rollander. I'm going up Gower Street, Karl, I can give you a lift if you like.

**KARL**. Thank you, Doctor.

**DOCTOR**. I'll wait downstairs in the car.

> *(He exits, closing the doors behind him.)*

**ANYA.** Karl, forgive me, Karl.

**KARL.** Forgive you, sweetheart? What is there to forgive?

**ANYA.** Everything. My moods, my bad temper. But it isn't really me, Karl. It's just the illness. You do understand?

**KARL.** *(Affectionately.)* I understand. Nothing you say will ever hurt me because I know your heart.

(**KARL** *clasps* **ANYA**'s *hand, she kisses it.*)

**ANYA.** Karl, you will be late for your lecture. You must go.

**KARL.** I wish I didn't have to leave you.

**ANYA.** Mrs. Roper will be back any minute and she will stay with me till Lisa gets back.

**HELEN.** I'm not going anywhere in particular, I can stay with Mrs. Hendryk till Miss Koletzky gets back.

**KARL.** Would you, Helen?

**HELEN.** Of course.

**KARL.** That's very kind of you.

*(He turns back to* **ANYA.***)*

Goodbye, darling.

**ANYA.** Good-bye.

**KARL.** Thank you, Helen.

*(He exits, closing the doors behind him. The daylight starts to fade.)*

**HELEN.** Is Miss Koletzky a relation?

**ANYA.** Yes, she's my first cousin. She came to England with us and has stayed with us ever since. This afternoon she has gone to see some friends who are passing through London. They are at the Hotel Russell, not very far away. It is so seldom we see friends from our own country.

**HELEN.** Would you like to go back?

**ANYA.** We cannot go back. A friend of my husband's, another professor, fell into disgrace because of his political views – he was arrested.

**HELEN.** How did that affect Professor Hendryk?

**ANYA.** His wife and children, you see, were left quite destitute. Professor Hendryk insisted that we should take them into our house. But when the authorities got to hear about it, they forced him to resign his position.

**HELEN.** Really, it didn't seem worth it, did it?

**ANYA.** That's what I felt, and I never liked Maria Schultz in the least. She was a most tiresome woman, always carping and criticising and moaning about something or other. And the children were very badly behaved and very destructive. It seems too bad that because of them we had to leave our nice home and come over here practically as refugees. This will never be home.

**HELEN.** It does seem rather tough luck on you.

**ANYA.** Men don't think of that. They only think of their ideas of what is right, or just, or one's duty.

**HELEN.** I know. Such an awful bore. But men aren't realists like we are.

*(There is a pause. A clock outside strikes four. **ANYA** looks at her watch.)*

**ANYA.** Lisa never gave me my medicine before she went out. She is very tiresome sometimes the way she forgets things.

**HELEN.** Can I do anything?

*(**ANYA** points to the shelves on the wall.)*

**ANYA.** It's on the little shelf over there. The little brown bottle. Four drops in water.

*(**HELEN** takes the bottle of medicine and a glass from the shelves.)*

It's for my heart, you know. There's a glass over there and a dropper. Be careful, it's very strong. That's why they keep it out of reach. Sometimes I feel so terribly depressed and I threaten to kill myself, and they think perhaps if I had it near me I'd yield to temptation and take an overdose.

*(**HELEN** takes the dropper from the bottle.)*

**HELEN.** You often want to, I suppose?

**ANYA.** *(Complacently.)* Oh, yes, one feels so often that one would be better dead.

**HELEN.** Yes, I can understand that.

**ANYA.** But, of course, one must be brave and go on.

> (**HELEN** *throws a quick glance at* **ANYA** *who is engrossed in her knitting. Tilting the bottle she empties the whole contents into the glass. She then adds some water and takes it to* **ANYA**.)

**HELEN.** Here you are.

**ANYA.** Thank you, my dear.

> *(She takes the glass and sips.)*

It tastes rather strong.

**HELEN.** Four drops, you said?

**ANYA.** Yes, that's right.

> *(She drinks it down quickly then puts the glass on the work-table.* **HELEN** *stands watching tensely.)*

The Professor works much too hard, you know. He takes more pupils than he ought to do. I wish – I wish he could have an easier life.

**HELEN.** Perhaps some day he will.

**ANYA.** I doubt it. *(Smiling.)* He's so good to everyone. So full of kindness. He is so good to me, so patient.

> *(She catches her breath.)*

Ah!

**HELEN.** What is it?

**ANYA.** Just – I don't seem to be able to get my breath. You're sure you didn't give me too much?

**HELEN.** I gave you the right dose.

**ANYA.** I'm sure – I'm sure you did. I didn't mean – I didn't think...

*(Her words get slower as she settles back almost as if she is about to sleep. Her hand comes up very slowly towards her heart.)*

How strange – how very – strange.

*(Her head drops. **HELEN** watches, now looking frightened.)*

**HELEN.** *(Quietly.)* Mrs. Hendryk.

*(Silence.)*

*(Louder.)* Mrs. Hendryk.

*(**HELEN** takes **ANYA**'s wrist and feels the pulse. Finding that it has stopped, she gasps and flings the hand down in horror. She stands staring for some moments then shakes herself back to reality. She sees the glass on the work-table, picks it up and wipes it on her handkerchief. Then leaning over, she puts it carefully into **ANYA**'s hand. She stops and leans against the sofa, staring. After some moments she pulls herself together again. She picks up the medicine bottle and dropper, wipes her fingerprints off, and then gently presses **ANYA**'s other hand round the bottle. She places it on the work-table and puts the dropper beside it. Looking around she moves quickly to the sofa and collects her bag and gloves. She starts to exit but stops suddenly and dashes to the shelf for the water jug. She wipes it with her handkerchief then puts it on the work-table. The sound of a barrel organ is heard off\*. **HELEN** flings open the door and exits through the hall and out the front door. The door is heard to slam. There is quite a*

---

\* A license to produce *Verdict* does not include a performance license for any third-party or copyrighted music. Licensees should create an original composition or use music in the public domain. For further information, please see Music Use Note on page 3.

*pause, then the front door is heard again.*
**MRS. ROPER** *pops her head in.)*

**MRS. ROPER.** I got the tea.

*(She withdraws and disappears to the kitchen. She reappears in the doorway, taking off her hat and coat.)*

And I got the bacon and a dozen boxes of matches. Isn't everything a price these days? I tried to get some kidneys for young Muriel's supper, ten pence each they were, and they looked like little shrunken heads. She'll have to have what the others have and like it. I keep telling her money doesn't grow on trees.

*(She exits to Anya's bedroom. There is a considerable pause, then the front door opens and closes.* **LISA** *enters from the hall.)*

**LISA.** Have I been long?

*(She glances at* **ANYA** *thinking she is asleep. She smiles and removes her coat then suddenly sees the empty medicine bottle on the worktable. She rushes to* **ANYA**.*)*

Anya?

*(She lifts* **ANYA**'s *head then takes her hand away, it falls. She picks up the medicine bottle.* **MRS. ROPER** *enters from Anya's bedroom.)*

**MRS. ROPER.** *(Startled.)* Oh, I didn't hear you come in, miss.

*(***LISA** *puts the bottle down quickly; startled by* **MRS. ROPER**'s *sudden appearance.)*

**LISA.** I didn't know you were here, Mrs. Roper.

**MRS. ROPER.** Is anything wrong?

**LISA.** Mrs. Hendryk – I think Mrs. Hendryk is dead.

*(She moves to the telephone, lifts the receiver and dials.* **MRS. ROPER** *moves slowly toward* **ANYA**. *She sees the empty medicine bottle*

*then turns in horror, staring at* **LISA.** **LISA** *is waiting impatiently for someone to answer her call. With her back to* **MRS. ROPER,** *she does not see the look.)*

# ACT II

## Scene One

*(Four days later. About midday. The room is empty. It is much the same as before except that Anya's wheelchair has gone. The doors are all closed. After a moment, **KARL** enters from the front door. He pauses for a moment and looks where Anya's wheelchair used to be, then sits heavily in the armchair. **LISA**, the **DOCTOR** and **LESTER** follow. They enter very solemnly.)*

**DOCTOR**. *(Uncomfortably.)* Well, that's over.

**LISA**. I have never been to an inquest in this country before. Are they always like that?

**DOCTOR**. Well, they vary, you know, they vary.

*(A pause.)*

**LISA**. It seems so business-like, so unemotional.

**DOCTOR**. Well, of course, we don't go in for emotion much. It's just a routine business enquiry, that's all.

**LESTER**. Wasn't it rather an odd sort of verdict? They said she died from an overdose of stropanthin but they didn't say how it was administered. I should have thought they'd have said suicide while the balance of the mind was disturbed and have done with it.

*(**KARL** rouses himself.)*

**KARL**. I cannot believe that Anya committed suicide.

**LISA**. *(Thoughtfully.)* I should not have said so, either.

**LESTER**. All the same, the evidence was pretty clear. Her fingerprints on the bottle and on the glass.

**KARL.** It must have been some kind of accident. Her hand shook a great deal, you know. She must have poured in far more than she realised. The curious thing is that I can't remember putting the bottle and glass beside her, yet I suppose I must have done.

**LISA.** It was my fault. I should have given her the drops before I went out.

**DOCTOR.** It was nobody's fault. Nothing is more unprofitable than accusing oneself of having left undone something one should have done or the opposite. These things happen and they're very sad. Let's leave it at that – *(Under his breath.)* – if we can.

**KARL.** You don't think Anya took an overdose, deliberately, Doctor?

**DOCTOR.** *(Slowly.)* I shouldn't have said so.

**LESTER.** She did talk about it you know. I mean, when she got depressed.

**DOCTOR.** Yes, yes, nearly all chronic invalids talk about suicide. They seldom commit it.

    *(A pause.)*

**LESTER.** *(Embarrassed.)* I say, I do hope I'm not butting in, coming here. I expect you want to be alone. I shouldn't...

**KARL.** No, no, my dear boy, it was kind of you.

**LESTER.** I just thought perhaps there was something I could do.

    *(A pause. He looks devoutly at **KARL**.)*

I'd do anything – if only I could do something to help.

**KARL.** Your sympathy helps. Anya was very fond of you, Lester.

    *(**MRS. ROPER** enters from the kitchen. She wears a rusty black costume and hat. She carries a tray of coffee and a plate of sandwiches.)*

**MRS. ROPER.** *(Quietly.)* I've made some coffee and some little sandwiches.

*(She puts the tray on the table then turns to* **KARL**.*)*

I thought, sir, as you'd need something to keep your strength up.

**KARL**. Thank you, Mrs. Roper.

*(**LISA** crosses to the tray and pours the coffee.)*

**MRS. ROPER**. I hurried back from the inquest as fast as I could sir, so as to have things ready when you come.

*(**KARL** realises Mrs. Roper's rather unusual costume.)*

**KARL**. Did you go to the inquest, then?

**MRS. ROPER**. 'Course I did. I felt I had an interest, like. Poor dear lady. Low in her spirits, wasn't she? I thought I'd go as a sign of respect, if nothing more. I can't say as it's been very nice, though, having the police here asking questions.

*(The others avoid looking at* **MRS. ROPER** *directly in the hope that she will stop talking and leave but she persists in trying to make conversation.)*

**DOCTOR**. These routine enquiries have to be made, Mrs. Roper.

*(He takes a cup of coffee to* **KARL** *then collects one for himself.)*

**MRS. ROPER**. Of course, sir.

**DOCTOR**. Whenever a certificate cannot be given, there has to be a coroner's enquiry.

**MRS. ROPER**. Oh, yes, sir, I'm sure it's very right and proper, but it's not very nice. That's what I say. It's not what I've been accustomed to. My husband, he wouldn't like it at all if I were mixed up in anything of that sort.

**LISA**. I don't see that you are mixed up in it in any way, Mrs. Roper.

**MRS. ROPER.** *(Eagerly.)* Well, they asked me questions, didn't they, as to whether she was low in her spirits and whether she'd ever talked about anything of the kind. Oh, quite a lot of questions they asked me.

**KARL.** *(Sharply.)* Well, that is all over now, Mrs. Roper. I don't think you need worry any further.

**MRS. ROPER.** *(Squashed.)* No, sir, thank you, sir.

> *(She exits through the hall to the kitchen, closing the doors behind her.)*

**DOCTOR.** All ghouls, you know, these women. Nothing they like better than illnesses, deaths, and funerals. An inquest, I expect, is an added joy.

**LISA.** Lester – coffee?

**LESTER.** Thanks so much.

> *(He helps himself to coffee.)*

**KARL.** It must have been some kind of accident, it must.

**DOCTOR.** I don't know.

> *(He sips his coffee.)*

Not quite the same as *your* coffee, Lisa, my dear.

**LISA.** I expect it's been boiling hard for half an hour.

**KARL.** It was kindly meant.

**LISA.** I wonder.

> *(She exits to Anya's bedroom, leaving the door open. The DOCTOR takes the plate of sandwiches from the tray to KARL.)*

**DOCTOR.** Have a sandwich?

**KARL.** No, thank you.

> *(The DOCTOR puts the sandwiches in front of LESTER.)*

**DOCTOR.** Finish them up, my boy. Always hungry at your age.

**LESTER.** Well, thanks. I don't mind if I do.

**LISA.** *(Offstage.)* Karl.

**KARL**. Excuse me a moment. *(Calling.)* Yes, I am coming.

> *(He exits to Anya's bedroom, closing the door behind him.)*

**LESTER**. He's terribly cut up, isn't he, Doctor?

> *(The* **DOCTOR** *takes out his pipe.)*

**DOCTOR**. Yes.

**LESTER**. It seems odd in a way, at least I don't mean odd, because, I suppose – what I mean is, it's so difficult to understand what other people feel like.

**DOCTOR**. Just what are you trying to say, my boy?

**LESTER**. Well, what I mean is, poor Mrs. Hendryk being an invalid and all that, you'd think, wouldn't you, that he'd get a bit impatient with her or feel himself tied. And you'd think that really, underneath, he'd be glad to be free. Not a bit. He loved her. He really loved her.

**DOCTOR**. Love isn't just glamour, desire, sex appeal – all the things you young people are so sure it is. That's nature's start of the whole business. It's the showy flower, if you like. But love's the root. Underground, out of sight, nothing much to look at, but it's where the life is.

**LESTER**. I suppose so, yes. But passion doesn't last, sir, does it?

**DOCTOR**. *(Despairingly.)* God give me strength. You young people know nothing about these things. You read in the papers of divorces, of love tangles with a sex angle to everything. Study the columns of deaths sometimes for a change. Plenty of records there of Emily this and John that dying in their seventy-fourth year, beloved wife of so-and-so, beloved husband of someone else. Unassuming records of lives spent together, sustained by the root I've just talked about which still puts out its leaves and its flowers. Not showy flowers, but still flowers.

**LESTER**. I suppose you're right. I've never thought about it. I've always thought that getting married is taking a bit of a chance, unless, of course, you meet a girl who...

**DOCTOR**. Yes, yes, that's the recognised pattern. You meet a girl – or you've already met a girl – who's different.

**LESTER**. *(Earnestly.)* But really, sir, she *is* different.

**DOCTOR**. *(Humorously.)* I see. Well, good luck to you, young fellow.

> (**KARL** *enters from Anya's bedroom. He carries a small pendant.*)

**KARL**. Will you give this to your daughter, Doctor? It was Anya's and I know she would like Margaret to have it.

> (*He hands the pendant to the* **DOCTOR**.)

**DOCTOR**. *(Moved.)* Thank you, Karl. I know Margaret will appreciate the gift.

> (*He puts the pendant in his wallet.*)

Well, I must be off. Can't keep my surgery patients waiting.

**LESTER**. I'll go, too, if you're sure there's nothing I can do for you, sir.

**KARL**. As a matter of fact there is.

> (**LESTER** *looks delighted.*)

Lisa has been making up some parcels of clothes and things like that – she is sending them to the East London Mission. If you would help her to carry them to the post office...

**LESTER**. Of course I will.

> (*He exits to Anya's bedroom.*)

**DOCTOR**. Good-bye, Karl.

> (*The* **DOCTOR** *exits through the hall and out the front door.* **LESTER** *enters from Anya's bedroom carrying a large box wrapped in brown paper. He takes it to the desk and fastens it with sellotape.* **LISA** *follows him carrying a drawer containing letters and a small trinket box.*)

**LISA**. If you would look through these, Karl.

*(She puts the drawer on the sofa.)*

Sit down here and go through these, quietly and alone. It has to be done and the sooner the better.

KARL. How wise you are, Lisa. One puts these things off and dreads them – dreads the hurt. As you say, it's better to do it and finish.

LISA. I shan't be long. Come along, Lester.

> *(LISA and LESTER exit, closing the doors behind them. KARL collects the wastepaper basket from the desk, sits on the sofa and puts the drawer on his knee. He starts to go through the letters.)*

KARL. *(Reading.)* So long ago, so long ago.

> *(The front door bell rings.)*

Oh, go away whoever you are.

MRS. ROPER. *(Offstage.)* Would you come inside, please.

> *(MRS. ROPER enters from the hall and stands to one side.)*

It's Miss Rollander, sir.

> *(HELEN enters. KARL rises and puts the drawer on the table. MRS. ROPER exits through the hall to the kitchen, leaving the doors open.)*

HELEN. I do hope I'm not being a nuisance. I went to the inquest, you see, and afterwards I thought I must come here and speak to you. But if you'd rather I went away...

KARL. No, no, it was kind of you.

> *(MRS. ROPER enters from the kitchen, putting on her coat.)*

MRS. ROPER. I'll just pop out and get another quarter of tea before he closes. We're right out again.

> *(KARL is far away, fingering the letters in the drawer.)*

KARL. Yes, of course, Mrs. Roper.

**MRS. ROPER**. Oh, I see what you're doing, sir. And a sad business it always is. My sister now, she's a widder. Kep' all her husband's letters, she did, what he wrote her from the Middle East. And she'll take them out and cry over them, like as not.

(**HELEN** *is rather impatient about* **MRS. ROPER***'s chatter.*)

The heart doesn't forget, sir, that's what I say. The heart doesn't forget.

**KARL**. As you say, Mrs. Roper.

**MRS. ROPER**. Must have been a terrible shock to you, sir, wasn't it? Or did you expect it?

**KARL**. No, I did not expect it.

**MRS. ROPER**. Can't imagine how she came to do such a thing.

(*She stares fascinated at the place where Anya's chair used to be.*)

It don't seem right, sir, not right at all.

**KARL**. (*Exasperated.*) Did you say you were going to get some tea, Mrs. Roper?

**MRS. ROPER**. That's right, sir, and I must hurry, sir because that grocer there, he shuts at half past twelve.

(*She exits, closing the doors behind her.*)

**HELEN**. I was so sorry to hear...

**KARL**. Thank you.

**HELEN**. Of course she'd been ill a long time, hadn't she? She must have got terribly depressed.

**KARL**. Did she say anything to you before you left her that day?

**HELEN**. (*Nervously.*) No, I – I don't think so. Nothing particular.

**KARL**. But she was depressed – in low spirits?

**HELEN**. Yes. Yes, she was.

**KARL.** *(Accusingly.)* You went away and left her – alone – before Lisa returned.

**HELEN.** *(Quickly.)* I'm sorry about that. I'm afraid it didn't occur to me. I mean, she said she was perfectly all right and she urged me not to stay, and – well, as a matter of fact, I – I thought she really wanted me to go – and so I did. Of course, now...

**KARL.** No, no. I understand. I can see that if my poor Anya had this in her mind she might have urged you to go.

**HELEN.** And in a way, really, it's the best thing that could have happened, isn't it?

**KARL.** *(Angrily.)* What do you mean – the best thing that could have happened?

**HELEN.** For you, I mean. And for her, too. She wanted to get out of it all, well, now she has. So everything is all right, isn't it?

**KARL.** It's difficult for me to believe that she did want to get out of it all.

**HELEN.** She said so – after all, she couldn't have been happy, could she?

**KARL.** *(Thoughtfully.)* Sometimes she was very happy.

**HELEN.** She couldn't have been, knowing she was a burden on you.

**KARL.** *(Heatedly.)* She was never a burden to me.

**HELEN.** Oh, why must you be so hypocritical about it all? I know you were kind to her and good to her, but let's face facts, to be tied to a querulous invalid is a drag on any man. Now, you're free. You can go ahead. You can do anything – anything. Aren't you ambitious?

**KARL.** I don't think so.

**HELEN.** But you are, of course you are. I've heard people talk about you. I've heard people say that that book of yours was the most brilliant of the century.

**KARL.** Fine words, indeed.

**HELEN.** And they were people who knew. You've had offers, too, to go to the United States, to all sorts of places.

Haven't you? You turned them down because of your wife whom you couldn't leave and who couldn't travel.

*(She approaches him.)*

HELEN. You've been tied so long, you hardly know what it is to feel free. Wake up, Karl, wake up. Be yourself. You did the best you could for Anya. Well, now it's over. You can start to enjoy yourself, to live life as it really ought to be lived.

KARL. Is this a sermon you're preaching me, Helen?

HELEN. It's only the present and the future that matter.

KARL. The present and the future are made up of the past.

HELEN. You're free. Why should we go on pretending we don't love each other?

KARL. *(Harshly.)* I don't love you, Helen, you must get that into your head. I don't love you. You're living in a fantasy of your own making.

HELEN. I'm not.

KARL. You are. I hate to be brutal, but I've got to tell you now I've no feelings for you of the kind you imagine.

HELEN. You must have. You must have. After what I've done for you. Some people wouldn't have had the courage, but I had. I loved you so much that I couldn't bear to see you tied to a useless querulous woman. You don't know what I'm talking about, do you? I killed her. Now, do you understand? I killed her.

KARL. *(Stupefied.)* You killed... I don't know what you're saying.

HELEN. I killed your wife. I'm not ashamed of it. People who are sick and worn out and useless should be removed so as to leave room for the ones who matter.

*(KARL backs away unable to take it in.)*

KARL. You killed Anya?

HELEN. She asked for her medicine. I gave it to her. I gave her the whole bottleful.

*(KARL backs further away, utterly aghast.)*

**KARL.** You – you…

**HELEN.** Don't worry. Nobody will ever know. I thought of everything.

> *(She speaks rather like a confident, pleased child as she approaches* **KARL**.*)*

I wiped off all the fingerprints, and put her own fingers first round the glass and then round the bottle. So that's all right, you see. I never really meant to tell you, but I just suddenly felt that I couldn't bear there to be any secrets between us.

> *(She lays her hands on* **KARL** *who pushes them away.)*

**KARL.** You killed Anya.

**HELEN.** If you once got used to the idea…

**KARL.** You – killed – Anya.

> *(Every time he repeats the words, his consciousness of her act grows greater and his tone more menacing. He seizes her suddenly by the shoulders and shakes her like a rat.)*

You miserable immature child – what have you done? Prating so glibly of your courage and your resource. You killed my wife – my Anya. Do you realise what you've done? Talking about things you don't understand, without conscience, without pity. I could take you by the neck and strangle you here and now.

> *(He seizes her by the throat and starts to strangle her.* **HELEN,** *struggling is forced backwards.* **KARL** *eventually flings her away and she falls, gasping for breath.)*

Get out of here. Get out before I do to you what you did to Anya.

> *(***HELEN** *still gasping for breath starts sobbing.* **KARL** *staggers back, near collapse.)*

**HELEN.** *(Desperately.)* Karl.

**KARL.** Get out. *(Shouting.)* Get out, I say.

(**HELEN** *rises, staggers, collects her handbag and gloves as in a trance then exits through the hall and out the front door.* **KARL** *buries his head in his hands. There is a pause then the front door is heard.* **LISA** *enters.*)

LISA. *(Calling.)* I'm back, Karl.

(*She exits to her bedroom.* **KARL** *crosses slowly to the sofa and almost collapses on to it.*)

KARL. My poor Anya.

(*There is a pause then* **LISA** *enters from her bedroom.*)

LISA. *(Casually.)* I met Helen on the stairs. She looked very strange. Went past me as though she didn't see me.

(*She sees* **KARL** *distraught.*)

Karl, what has happened?

KARL. *(Simply.)* She killed *Anya.*

LISA. *(Startled.)* What!

KARL. She killed Anya. Anya asked for her medicine and that miserable child gave her an overdose deliberately.

LISA. But Anya's fingerprints were on the glass.

KARL. Helen put them there after she was dead.

(*Trying to deal with the situation,* **LISA** *attempts to remain calm and matter-of-fact.*)

LISA. I see – she thought of everything.

KARL. I knew. I always knew that Anya wouldn't have killed herself.

LISA. She's in love with you, of course.

KARL. Yes, yes. But I never gave her any reason to believe that I cared for her. I didn't, Lisa, I swear I didn't.

LISA. I don't suppose you did. She's the type of girl who would assume that whatever she wanted must be so.

KARL. My poor, brave Anya.

(*There is a long pause.*)

**LISA**. What are you going to do about it?

**KARL**. *(Surprised.)* Do?

**LISA**. Aren't you going to report it to the police?

**KARL**. *(Startled.)* Tell the police?

   (**LISA** *still tries to remain calm.*)

**LISA**. It's murder, you know.

**KARL**. Yes, it was murder.

**LISA**. Well, you must report what she said to the police.

**KARL**. I can't do that.

**LISA**. Why not? Do you condone murder?

**KARL**. But I can't let that girl...

   (**LISA** *has to restrain herself.*)

**LISA**. We've come of our own accord, as refugees, to a country where we live under the protection of its laws. I think we should respect its law, no matter what our own feelings on the subject may be.

**KARL**. You seriously think I should go to the police?

**LISA**. Yes.

**KARL**. Why?

**LISA**. It seems to me pure common sense.

**KARL**. Common sense! Common sense! Can one rule one's life by common sense?

**LISA**. You don't, I know. You never have. You're soft-hearted, Karl. I'm not.

**KARL**. Is it wrong to feel pity? Can mercy ever be wrong?

**LISA**. It can lead to a lot of unhappiness.

**KARL**. One must be prepared to suffer for one's principles.

**LISA**. Perhaps. That is your business. But other people suffer for them as well. Anya suffered for them.

**KARL**. I know, I know. But you don't understand.

   (**LISA** *faces* **KARL**.)

**LISA**. I understand very well.

**KARL**. What do you want me to do?

LISA. I have told you. Go to the police. Anya has been murdered. This girl has admitted to murdering her. The police must be told.

KARL. You haven't thought, Lisa. The girl is so young. She is only twenty-three.

LISA. Whereas Anya was thirty-eight.

KARL. If she is tried and condemned – what good will it do? Can it bring Anya back? Don't you see, Lisa, revenge can't bring Anya back to life again.

LISA. No. Anya is dead.

(*KARL sits on the sofa, distraught.*)

KARL. I wish you could see it my way.

LISA. I can't see it your way. I loved Anya. We were cousins and friends. We went about as girls together. I looked after her when she was ill. I know how she tried to be brave, how she tried not to complain. I know how difficult life was for her.

KARL. Going to the police won't bring Anya back.

(*LISA does not answer.*)

And don't you see, Lisa, I'm bound to feel responsible, myself. I must in some way have encouraged the girl.

LISA. You didn't encourage her.

(*She kneels, facing* KARL.)

Let's speak plainly. She did her utmost to seduce you, and failed.

KARL. No matter how you put it, I feel responsible. Love for me was her motive.

LISA. Her motive was to get what she wanted, as she always has got everything she wanted all her life.

KARL. That's just what has been her tragedy. She has never had a chance.

LISA. And she's young and beautiful.

KARL. (*Sharply.*) What do you mean?

**LISA**. I wonder if you'd be so tender if she were one of your plain girl students.

**KARL**. *(Rising.)* You can't think...

**LISA**. *(Rising.)* What can't I think?

**KARL**. That I want that girl...

**LISA**. Why not? Aren't you attracted to her? Be honest with yourself. Are you sure you're not really a little in love with the girl?

**KARL**. You can say that? You? When you know – when you've always known...? It's *you* I love. You! I lie awake at night thinking about you, longing for you. Lisa, Lisa...

> (**KARL** *takes* **LISA** *in his arms. They kiss passionately. A shadowy figure, whose identity should remain unknown, is seen in the doorway to the hall. After a pause, the front door closes with a bang.* **KARL** *and* **LISA** *move apart, panicked. They look to the door.)*

## Scene Two

*(Six hours later. Evening. The room is in darkness. **LISA** is seated on the sofa smoking. She is almost invisible. The sound of voices are heard in the hall as the front door opens and closes. **KARL** enters; he has a newspaper in his overcoat pocket. The **DOCTOR** follows him on.)*

**KARL.** Nobody's at home. I wonder...

*(The **DOCTOR** switches on the lights; they see **LISA**.)*

**DOCTOR.** Lisa! Why are you sitting here in the dark?

**LISA.** I was just thinking.

*(**KARL** goes to the desk chair and puts his coat over the back of it.)*

**DOCTOR.** I met Karl at the end of the street and we came along together. D'you know what I prescribe for you, Karl? A little alcohol. A stiff brandy, eh, Lisa?

*(**LISA** makes a slight move.)*

No – I know my way about.

*(He goes to the cupboard, takes out a bottle of brandy and a glass then pours a stiff drink.)*

He's had a shock, you know. A bad shock.

**KARL.** I have told him about Helen.

**DOCTOR.** Yes, he told me.

**LISA.** It's not been such a shock to you, I gather?

**DOCTOR.** I've been worried, you know. I didn't think Anya was a suicidal type and I couldn't see any possibility of an accident.

*(He gives **KARL** the brandy.)*

And then the inquest aroused my suspicions. Clearly the police were behind the verdict. Yes, it looked fishy. The police questioned me fairly closely and I couldn't help seeing what they were driving at. Of course, they didn't actually say anything.

LISA. So you were not surprised?

DOCTOR. No, not really. That young woman thought she could get away with anything. Even murder. Well, she was wrong.

KARL. *(Quietly.)* I feel responsible.

DOCTOR. Karl, take it from me, you weren't responsible in any way. Compared to that young woman you're an innocent in arms. Anyway, the whole thing's out of your hands now.

LISA. You think he should go to the police?

DOCTOR. Yes.

KARL. No.

DOCTOR. Because you insist on feeling partly responsible? You're too sensitive.

KARL. Poor wretched child.

DOCTOR. Callous, murdering little bitch! That's nearer the mark. And I shouldn't worry before you need. Ten to one it'll never come to an arrest. Presumably she'll deny everything – and there's got to be evidence, you know. The police may be quite sure who's done a thing but be unable to make out a case. The girl's father is a very important person. One of the richest men in England. That counts.

KARL. There I think you are wrong.

DOCTOR. Oh, I'm not saying anything against the police. If they've got a case, they'll go ahead without fear or favour. All I mean is that they'll have to scrutinise their evidence with extra care. And on the face of it there can't really be much evidence, you know. Unless, of course, she breaks down and confesses the whole thing. And I should imagine she's much too hard-boiled for that.

KARL. She confessed to me.

**DOCTOR.** That's different. Though as a matter of fact I can't see why she did. Seems to me a damn silly thing to do.

**LISA.** Because she was proud of it.

*(The **DOCTOR** looks curiously at her.)*

**DOCTOR.** You think so?

**KARL.** It is true – that's what is so terrible.

*(The front door bell rings.)*

Who can that be?

**DOCTOR.** One of your boys or girls, I expect. I'll get rid of them.

*(The **DOCTOR** exits through the hall to the front door. **KARL** rises and puts his glass on the desk.)*

**OGDEN.** *(Offstage.)* Could I see Professor Hendryk, please?

**DOCTOR.** *(Offstage.)* Would you come this way, please.

*(The **DOCTOR** enters and stands to one side.)*

It's Inspector Ogden.

**(DETECTIVE INSPECTOR OGDEN** *and* **POLICE SERGEANT PEARCE** *enter.* **OGDEN** *has a pleasant manner and a poker face. The* **SERGEANT** *closes the doors, then stands to one side.)*

**OGDEN.** *(Pleasantly.)* I hope we're not disturbing you, Professor Hendryk.

**KARL.** Not at all.

**OGDEN.** Good evening, Miss Koletzky. I expect you didn't think you would see me again – but we have a few more questions to ask. It was an open verdict, you understand. Insufficient evidence as to how the deceased lady came to take the fatal dose.

**KARL.** I know.

**OGDEN.** Have your own ideas changed as to that, sir, since we first talked about it?

(**KARL** *looks quickly at* **LISA**. *There is a pause.*
**OGDEN** *and the* **SERGEANT** *note the exchanged
glance.*)

**KARL**. *(Deliberately.)* They have not changed. I still think it
must have been some sort of – accident.

(**LISA** *turns away. The* **DOCTOR** *almost snorts
and turns aside.*)

**OGDEN**. But definitely not suicide.

**KARL**. Definitely not suicide.

**OGDEN**. Well, you're quite right as to that, sir. It was not
suicide.

*(They all look at* **OGDEN**.*)*

**LISA**. *(Quietly.)* How do you know?

**OGDEN**. By evidence that was not given at the inquest.
Evidence as to the fingerprints found on the bottle
containing the fatal drug – and on the glass, also.

**KARL**. You mean... But they were my wife's fingerprints,
weren't they?

**OGDEN**. Oh, yes, sir. They were your wife's fingerprints.
*(Softly.)* But *she* didn't make them.

*(The* **DOCTOR** *and* **KARL** *exchange looks.)*

**KARL**. What do you mean?

**OGDEN**. It's the sort of thing that an amateur criminal
thinks is so easy. To pick up a person's hand and close
it round a gun or a bottle or whatever it may be. But
actually it's not so easy to do. The position of those
fingerprints is such that they couldn't have been made
by a living woman grasping a bottle. That means that
*somebody else* took your wife's hand and folded the
fingers round the bottle and the glass so as to give the
impression that your wife committed suicide. A rather
childish piece of reasoning and done by someone
rather cocksure of their own ability. Also, there ought
to have been plenty of other prints on the bottle, but

there weren't – it had been wiped clean before your wife's were applied. You see what that means?

KARL. I see what it means.

OGDEN. There would be no reason to do such a thing if it was an accident. That only leaves one possibility.

KARL. Yes.

OGDEN. I wonder if you do see, sir. It means – an ugly word – murder.

KARL. Murder.

OGDEN. Doesn't that seem very incredible to you, sir?

> (KARL *speaks more to himself than* OGDEN.)

KARL. You cannot know how incredible. My wife was a very sweet and gentle woman. It will always seem to me both terrible and unbelievable that anyone should have – killed her.

OGDEN. You yourself...

KARL. *(Sharply.)* Are you accusing me?

OGDEN. Of course not, sir. If I'd any suspicions concerning you, I should give you the proper warning. No, Professor Hendryk, we've checked your story and your time is fully accounted for. You left here in the company of Dr. Stoner and he states that there was no medicine bottle or glass on your wife's table at that time. Between the time you left and the time Miss Koletzky says she arrived here and found your wife dead, every moment of your time is accounted for. You were lecturing to a group of students at the university. No, there is no suggestion of your having been the person to put the fingerprints on the glass. What I am asking you, sir, is whether you have any idea yourself as to who could have done so?

> (*There is quite a long pause.* KARL *stares fixedly ahead of him.*)

KARL. I –

> (*He pauses.*)

– cannot help you.

(**OGDEN** *exchanges glances with the* **SERGEANT.**)

**OGDEN.** You will appreciate, of course, that this alters things. I wonder if I might have a look round the flat. Round Mrs. Hendryk's bedroom in particular. I can get a search warrant if necessary, but...

**KARL.** Of course. Look anywhere you please. My wife's bedroom is through there.

(*He indicates the door to Anya's bedroom.*)

**OGDEN.** Thank you.

**KARL.** Miss Koletzky has been sorting through her things.

(**LISA** *opens the door to Anya's bedroom.* **OGDEN** *and the* **SERGEANT** *exit. She looks at* **KARL** *then follows them off, closing the door behind her.*)

**DOCTOR.** I've known you long enough, Karl, to tell you plainly that you're being a fool.

**KARL.** I can't be the one to put them on her track. They'll get her soon enough without my help.

**DOCTOR.** I'm not so sure of that. And it's all highfalutin' nonsense.

**KARL.** She didn't know what she was doing.

**DOCTOR.** She knew perfectly.

**KARL.** She didn't know what she was doing because life has not yet taught her understanding and compassion.

(**LISA** *enters from Anya's bedroom, closing the door behind her. She turns to the* **DOCTOR.**)

**LISA.** Have you made him see sense?

**DOCTOR.** Not yet.

(**LISA** *shivers.*)

You're cold.

**LISA.** No – I'm not cold. I'm afraid. I shall make some coffee.

(**LISA** *exits through the hall to the kitchen.*)

**KARL**. I wish I could get you and Lisa to see that revenge will not bring Anya back to life again.

**DOCTOR**. And suppose our little beauty goes on disposing of wives that happen to stand in her way?

**KARL**. I will not believe that.

> (*The* **SERGEANT** *and* **OGDEN** *enter from Anya's bedroom.*)

**OGDEN**. I gather some of your wife's clothing and effects have already been disposed of?

**KARL**. Yes. They were sent off to the East London Mission, I think.

> (*The* **SERGEANT** *makes a note.*)

**OGDEN**. What about papers, letters?

**KARL**. I was going through them this morning.

> (*He indicates the little drawer.*)

Though what you expect to find...

**OGDEN**. One never knows. Some note, a memorandum set down...

**KARL**. I doubt it. Still, look through them, of course, if you must. I don't expect you'll find...

> (*He stops and picks up a bundle of letters tied with ribbon.*)

Will you need these? They are the letters I wrote to my wife many years ago.

**OGDEN**. (*Gently.*) I'm afraid I must just look through them.

> (*He takes the letters from* **KARL**. *There is quite a pause then* **KARL** *turns impatiently towards the doors to the hall.*)

**KARL**. I shall be in the kitchen if you want me, Inspector Ogden.

(**KARL** *exits through the hall to the kitchen. The* **DOCTOR** *follows him off, closing the doors behind him.*)

**SERGEANT.** Do you think he was in on it?

**OGDEN.** No, I don't.

(*He starts to go through the papers in the drawer.*)

Not beforehand. Hadn't the faintest idea, I should say. (*Grimly.*) But he knows now – and it's been a shock to him.

**SERGEANT.** He's not saying anything.

**OGDEN.** No. That would be too much to expect. Doesn't seem to be much here. Not likely to be, under the circumstances.

**SERGEANT.** If there had been, our Mrs. Mop would have known about it. I'd say she was a pretty good snooper. That kind always knows the dirt. And did she enjoy spilling it!

**OGDEN.** (*Distastefully.*) An unpleasant woman.

**SERGEANT.** She'll do all right in the witness-box.

**OGDEN.** Unless she overdoes it. Well, nothing additional here. We'd better get on with the job.

(*He moves to the doors to the hall, opens one and calls:.*)

Will you come in here, please.

(**LISA,** *the* **DOCTOR** *and* **KARL** *enter from the kitchen. The* **SERGEANT** *moves to the doors, closes them, then stands guard in front.*)

Miss Koletzky, there are some additional questions I would like to ask you. You understand that you are not forced to answer anything unless you please.

**LISA.** I do not want to answer any questions.

**OGDEN.** Perhaps you're wise. Lisa Koletzky, I arrest you on the charge of administering poison to Anya Hendryk on March the fifth last and it is my duty to warn you that anything you say will be taken down and may be used in evidence.

KARL. *(Horror-struck.)* What's this? What are you doing? What are you saying?

OGDEN. Please, Professor Hendryk, don't let's have a scene.

(KARL *guardedly moves in front of* LISA.)

KARL. But you can't arrest Lisa, you can't, you can't. She's done nothing.

(LISA *gently pushes* KARL *aside and speaks in a loud, clear, calm voice.*)

LISA. I did not murder my cousin.

OGDEN. You'll have plenty of opportunity to say everything you want, later.

(KARL, *losing restraint, advances on* OGDEN *but the* DOCTOR *holds him back.*)

KARL. *(Shouting.)* You can't do this. You can't.

(*Ignoring him,* OGDEN *turns to* LISA.)

OGDEN. If you need a coat or a hat...

LISA. I need nothing.

(LISA *looks at* KARL *for a moment, then turns. The* SERGEANT *opens the door.* LISA *exits down the hall.* OGDEN *and the* SERGEANT *follow her off.* KARL *suddenly makes a decision and runs after them.*)

KARL. Inspector Ogden! Come back. I must speak to you.

OGDEN. *(Offstage.)* Wait in the hall, Sergeant.

SERGEANT. *(Offstage.)* Yes, sir.

(OGDEN *enters.*)

OGDEN. Yes, Professor Hendryk?

KARL. I have something to tell you. I know who killed my wife. It was not Miss Koletzky.

OGDEN. *(Politely.)* Who was it, then?

**KARL**. It was a girl called Helen Rollander. She is one of my pupils. She – she formed an unfortunate attachment to me. She was alone with my wife on the day in question, and she gave her an overdose of the heart medicine.

**OGDEN**. How do you know this, Professor Hendryk?

**KARL**. She told me herself, this morning.

**OGDEN**. Indeed? Were there any witnesses?

**KARL**. No, but I am telling you the truth.

**OGDEN**. *(Thoughtfully.)* Helen – Rollander. You mean the daughter of Sir William Rollander?

**KARL**. Yes. Her father is William Rollander. He is an important man. Does that make any difference?

**OGDEN**. No, it wouldn't make any difference – if your story were true.

**KARL**. I swear to you that it's true.

**OGDEN**. You are very devoted to Miss Koletzky, aren't you?

**KARL**. Do you think I would make up a story just to protect her?

**OGDEN**. I think it is quite possible – you are on terms of intimacy with Miss Koletzky, aren't you?

**KARL**. *(Dumbfounded.)* What do you mean?

**OGDEN**. Let me tell you, Professor Hendryk, that your daily woman, Mrs. Roper, came along to the police station this afternoon and made a statement.

**KARL**. Then it was Mrs. Roper who...

**OGDEN**. It is partly because of that statement that Miss Koletzky has been arrested.

**KARL**. You believe that Lisa and I...

**OGDEN**. Your wife was an invalid. Miss Koletzky is an attractive young woman. You were thrown together.

**KARL**. You think we planned together to kill Anya.

**OGDEN**. No, I don't think you planned it. I may be wrong there, of course. I think all the planning was done by Miss Koletzky. There was a prospect of your wife regaining her health owing to a new treatment. I think Miss Koletzky was taking no chance of that happening.

**KARL.** But I tell you that it was Helen Rollander.

**OGDEN.** You tell me, yes. It seems to me a most unlikely story. Is it plausible that a girl like Miss Rollander who's got the world at her feet and who hardly knows you, would do a thing like that? Making up an accusation of that kind reflects little credit on you, Professor Hendryk – trumping it up on the spur of the moment because you think it cannot be contradicted.

**KARL.** Listen. Go to Miss Rollander. Tell her that another woman has been arrested for the murder. Tell her, from me, that I know – *know* – that with all her faults, she is decent and honest. I swear that she will confirm what I have told you.

**OGDEN.** You've thought it up very cleverly, haven't you?

**KARL.** What do you mean?

**OGDEN.** What I say. But there's no-one who can confirm your story.

**KARL.** Only Helen herself.

**OGDEN.** Exactly.

**KARL.** And Dr. Stoner knows. I told him.

**OGDEN.** He knows because you told him.

**DOCTOR.** I believe it to be the truth, Inspector Ogden. If you remember, I mentioned to you that when we left Mrs. Hendryk that day, Miss Rollander remained behind to keep her company.

**OGDEN.** A kind offer on her part. We interviewed Miss Rollander at the time and I see no reason to doubt her story. She stayed for a short time and then Mrs. Hendryk asked her to leave since she felt tired.

**KARL.** Go to Helen now. Tell her what has happened. Tell her what I have asked you to tell her.

(**OGDEN** *ignores* **KARL**.)

**OGDEN**. Just when did Professor Hendryk tell you that Miss Rollander had killed his wife? Within the last hour, I should imagine.

**DOCTOR**. That is so.

**KARL**. We met in the street.

**OGDEN**. Didn't it strike you that if this was true, he would have come to us as soon as she admitted to him what she had done?

**DOCTOR**. He's not that kind of man.

**OGDEN**. *(Ruthlessly.)* I don't think you're really aware what kind of man he is.

*(He moves to Karl's coat on the desk chair.)*

He's a quick and clever thinker, and he's not overly scrupulous.

*(**KARL** starts towards **OGDEN**, but the **DOCTOR** quickly restrains him.)*

This is your coat and an evening paper, I see.

*(He draws paper from the pocket.)*

**KARL**. Yes, I bought it on the corner, just before I came in. I haven't had time to read it, yet.

**OGDEN**. Are you sure?

**KARL**. Yes – I am quite sure.

**OGDEN**. I think you did.

*(He reads from the paper.)*

"Sir William Rollander's only daughter, Helen Rollander, was the victim of a regrettable accident this morning. In crossing the road she was knocked down by a lorry. The lorry driver claims that Miss Rollander gave him no time to brake. She walked straight into the road without looking right or left, and was killed instantly."

*(**KARL** slumps on to the sofa.)*

I think that when you saw that paragraph, Professor Hendryk, you saw a way out to save your mistress by

accusing a girl who could never refute what you said –
because she was dead.

## Scene Three

*(Two months later. Late afternoon.* **KARL** *is seated on the sofa. The* **DOCTOR** *is reading the book of prose by Walter Savage Landor.* **LESTER** *is pacing. The telephone rings. They all start.* **LESTER**, *who is nearest to the telephone, lifts the receiver.)*

LESTER. Hello? ...No.

*(He replaces the receiver.)*

These reporters never stop.

KARL. I wish I had stayed in court. Why didn't you let me stay?

DOCTOR. Lisa specifically asked that you shouldn't remain in court to hear the verdict. We've got to respect her wish.

KARL. You could have stayed.

DOCTOR. She wanted me to be with you. The lawyers will let us know at once...

KARL. They can't find her guilty. They can't.

LESTER. If you'd like me to go back there...

DOCTOR. You stay here, Lester.

LESTER. If I'm any use. If there's anything I could do...

DOCTOR. You can answer that damn telephone that keeps ringing.

KARL. Yes, my dear boy. Stay. Your presence here helps me.

LESTER. Does it? Does it, really?

KARL. She must be, she will be acquitted. I can't believe that innocence can go unrecognised.

DOCTOR. Can't you? I can. One's seen it often enough. And you've seen it, Karl, time and time again. Mind you, I think she made a good impression on the jury.

LESTER. But the evidence was pretty damning. It's that frightful Roper woman. The things she said.

DOCTOR. She believed what she was saying, of course. That's what made her so unshakeable under cross-examination. It's particularly unfortunate that she should have seen you and Lisa embracing each other on the day of the inquest. She did see it, I suppose?

KARL. Yes, she must have seen it. It was true. It's the first time I have ever kissed Lisa.

DOCTOR. And a thoroughly bad time to choose. It's really a thousand pities that snooping woman never saw or heard anything that passed between you and Helen. "A very nice young lady" – that's all she had to say.

KARL. It is so odd to tell the truth and not be believed.

DOCTOR. All you've done is to bring down a lot of odium on yourself, for cooking up a scurrilous story about a girl who is dead.

KARL. If I'd only gone to the police right away, the moment she'd told me...

DOCTOR. If only you had. It's particularly unfortunate that you only came out with the story after you'd bought a paper containing the news that she's dead. And your reasons for not going to the police didn't sound credible in the least. Though they are to me, of course, because I know the incredible fool you are. The whole set of circumstances is thoroughly damnable. The Roper woman coming in to find Lisa standing by the body and holding the bottle in gloved fingers. The whole thing has built itself up in the most incredible fashion.

*(The telephone rings.)*

KARL. Is that...? Can it...?

*(There is a moment's agonising pause, then the DOCTOR motions to LESTER who goes to the telephone and lifts the receiver.)*

LESTER. Yes? ...Hello? ...Go to hell!

*(He slams the receiver down.)*

DOCTOR. Ghouls, that's what they are, ghouls.

**KARL.** If they find her guilty, if they...

**DOCTOR.** Well, we can appeal, you know.

**KARL.** Why should she have to go through all this? Why should she be the one to suffer? I wish I were in her place.

**DOCTOR.** Yes, it's always easier when it's oneself.

**KARL.** After all, I'm partly responsible for what happened...

**DOCTOR.** *(Interrupting.)* I've told you that's nonsense.

**KARL.** But Lisa has done nothing. Nothing.

> *(There is a long pause. The **DOCTOR** turns to **LESTER**.)*

**DOCTOR.** Go and make us some coffee, boy – if you know how.

**LESTER.** *(Indignantly.)* Of course I know how.

> *(The telephone rings. **LESTER** makes a move to answer it but **KARL** stops him.)*

Don't answer it.

> *(**LESTER** hesitates then exits through the hall to the kitchen. The telephone goes on ringing. **KARL** eventually rushes to it and picks up the receiver.)*

Leave me alone, can't you. Leave me alone.

> *(He slams down the receiver and sinks into the desk chair.)*

I can't bear it. I can't bear it.

**DOCTOR.** Patience, Karl. Courage.

**KARL.** What good is it saying that to me?

**DOCTOR.** Not much, but there's nothing else to say, is there? There's nothing that can help you now except courage.

**KARL.** I keep thinking of Lisa. Of what she must be suffering.

**DOCTOR.** I know, I know.

**KARL.** She's so brave. So wonderfully brave.

DOCTOR. Lisa is a very wonderful person. I have always known that.

KARL. I love her. Did you know I loved her?

DOCTOR. Yes, of course I knew. You've loved her for a long time.

KARL. Yes. Neither of us ever acknowledged it, but we knew. It didn't mean that I didn't love Anya. I did love Anya. I shall always love her. I didn't want her to die.

DOCTOR. I know, I know. I've never doubted that.

KARL. It's strange, perhaps, but one can love two women at the same time.

DOCTOR. Not at all strange. It often happens. And you know what Anya used to say to me? "When I'm gone, Karl must marry Lisa." That's what she used to say. "You must make him do it, Doctor," she used to say. "Lisa will look after him and be good to him. If he doesn't think of it you must put it into his head." That's what she used to say to me. I promised her that I would.

KARL. Tell me, really, Doctor. Do you think they'll acquit her? Do you?

DOCTOR. *(Gently.)* I think – you ought to prepare yourself...

KARL. Even her counsel didn't believe me, did he? He pretended to, of course, but he didn't believe me.

DOCTOR. No, I don't think he did, but – there are one or two sensible people on the jury – I think. That fat woman in the funny hat listened to every word you were saying about Helen, and I noticed her nodding her head in complete agreement. She probably has a husband who went off the rails with a young girl. You never know what queer things influence people.

> *(The telephone rings.)*

KARL. This time it must be.

> *(The **DOCTOR** moves to the telephone and lifts the receiver.)*

DOCTOR. Hello? ...

(**LESTER** *enters from the kitchen carrying a tray of coffee.*)

**KARL.** Well?

**LESTER.** Is that...?

(*He puts the tray on the table and starts to pour. The* **DOCTOR** *shouts into the telephone.*)

**DOCTOR.** No...no, I'm afraid he can't.

(*He slams down the receiver.*)

Another of the ghouls.

**KARL.** What can they hope to get out of it?

**DOCTOR.** Increased circulation, I suppose.

(**LESTER** *hands a cup of coffee to* **KARL.**)

**LESTER.** I hope it's all right. It took me some time to find everything.

**KARL.** Thank you.

(**LESTER** *hands a cup of coffee to the* **DOCTOR**, *then takes his own. They sip in silence.*)

**DOCTOR.** Have you ever seen herons flying low over a river bank?

**LESTER.** No, I don't think I have. Why?

**DOCTOR.** No reason.

**LESTER.** What put it into your head?

**DOCTOR.** I've no idea. Just wishing, I suppose, that all this wasn't true and that I was somewhere else.

**LESTER.** Yes, I can see that. It's so awful, not being able to do anything.

**DOCTOR.** Nothing's so bad as waiting.

(*A pause.*)

**LESTER.** I don't believe, you know, that I've ever seen a heron.

**DOCTOR.** Very graceful birds.

**KARL.** Doctor, I want you to do something for me.

**DOCTOR.** Yes? What is it?

**KARL**. I want you to go back to the court.

**DOCTOR**. No, Karl.

**KARL**. Yes, I know that you promised. But I want you to go back.

**DOCTOR**. Karl – Lisa...

**KARL**. If the worst happens, I would like Lisa to be able to see you there. And if it isn't the worst – well, then she'll need someone to look after her, to get her away, to bring her here.

> (*The* **DOCTOR** *stares at* **KARL** *for a moment.*)

I know I'm right.

**DOCTOR**. (*Deciding.*) Very well.

**LESTER**. I can stay and...

> (**KARL** *looks at the* **DOCTOR** *and shakes his head very slightly. The* **DOCTOR** *is quick to take the hint.*)

**DOCTOR**. No, you come with me, Lester. There are times when a man has got to be alone. That's right, isn't it, Karl?

**KARL**. Don't worry about me. I want to stay here quietly with Anya.

**DOCTOR**. What did you say? With Anya?

**KARL**. Did I say that? That's what it seems like. Leave me here. I shan't answer the telephone if it rings. I shall wait now until you come.

> (**LESTER** *exits followed by the* **DOCTOR** *who closes the doors behind him. The clock chimes six.*)

"While the light lasts I shall remember, And in the darkness I shall not forget."

> (*There is a pause then the telephone rings.* **KARL** *ignores it. He collects the coffee cups and takes them to the tray. He then exits with it down the hall to the kitchen. While he is off, the telephone stops ringing.* **KARL**

*re-enters, leaving the doors open. He pauses for a moment, staring at* **ANYA***'s work-table, then goes to the record cabinet and takes the Rachmaninoff record from it. He goes to the desk, sits, and puts the record in front of him.* **LISA** *suddenly enters. She comes down the hall, shuts the doors and leans against them.* **KARL** *turns.)*

Lisa! Lisa!

*(He rises, hardly believing his eyes.)*

Is it true? Is it?

**LISA.** They found me not guilty.

**KARL.** Oh, my darling, I'm so thankful. No-one shall ever hurt you again, Lisa.

*(He attempts to take her in his arms but she pushes him away.)*

**LISA.** No.

*(***KARL*** realises her coldness.)*

**KARL** What do you mean?

**LISA.** I've come here to get my things.

*(***KARL*** backs away.)*

**KARL.** What do you mean – your things?

**LISA.** Just a few things that I need. Then I am going away.

**KARL.** What do you mean – going away?

**LISA.** I'm leaving here.

**KARL.** But surely – that's ridiculous! D'you mean because of what people would say? Does that matter now?

**LISA.** You don't understand. I am going away for good.

**KARL.** Going away – where?

**LISA.** What does it matter? Somewhere. I can get a job. There'll be no difficulty about that. I may go abroad. I may stay in England. Wherever I go I'm starting a new life.

**KARL.** A new life? You mean – without me?

**LISA.** Yes. Yes, Karl. That's just what I mean. Without you.

**KARL.** But why? Why?

**LISA.** Because I've had enough.

**KARL.** I don't understand you.

**LISA.** We're not made to understand each other. We don't see things the same way, and I'm afraid of you.

**KARL.** How can you be afraid of me?

**LISA.** Because you're the kind of man who always brings suffering.

**KARL.** No.

**LISA.** It's true.

**KARL.** No.

**LISA.** I see people as they are. Without malice and without entering into judgment, but without illusions, either. I don't expect people to be wonderful or life to be wonderful, and I don't particularly want to be wonderful myself. If there are fields of amaranth – they can be on the other side of the grave as far as I am concerned.

**KARL.** Fields of amaranth? What are you talking about?

**LISA.** I'm talking about you, Karl. You put ideas first, not people. Ideas of loyalty and friendship and pity. And because of that the people who are near, suffer. You knew you'd lose your job if you befriended the Schultzes. And you knew, you must have known, what an unhappy life that would mean for Anya. But you didn't care about Anya. You only cared about your ideas of what was right. But people matter, Karl. They matter as much as ideas. Anya mattered, I matter. Because of your ideas, because of your mercy and compassion for the girl who killed your wife, you sacrificed *me. I* was the one who paid for your compassion. But I'm not ready to do that any more. I love you, but love isn't enough. You've more in common with the girl Helen than you have with me. She was like you – ruthless. She went all out for the things she believed in. She didn't care what happened to people as long as she got her own way.

**KARL.** Lisa, you can't mean what you are saying. You can't.

**LISA.** I do mean it. I've been thinking it really for a long time. I've thought of it all these days in court. I didn't really think they'd acquit me. I don't know why they did. The judge didn't seem to think there was much reasonable doubt. But I suppose some of the jury believed me. There was one little man who kept on looking at me as though he was sizing me up. Just a commonplace ordinary little man – but he looked at me and thought I hadn't done it – or perhaps he thought I was the kind of woman that he'd like to go to bed with and he didn't want me to suffer. I don't know what he thought – but – he was a *person* looking at another *person*, and he was on my side and perhaps he persuaded the others. And so I'm free. I've been given a second chance to start life again. I'm starting again – alone.

  (**LISA** *exits to Anya's bedroom.*)

**KARL.** (*Pleadingly.*) Lisa. You can't mean it. You can't be so cruel. You must listen. Lisa. I implore you.

  (**LISA** *re-enters carrying a small silver photo frame.*)

**LISA.** No, Karl. What happens to the women who love you? Anya loved you and she died. Helen loved you and she's dead. I – have been very near death. I've had enough. I want to be free of you – for ever.

**KARL.** But where will you go?

  (*There is a pause.*)

**LISA.** You told me to go away and marry and have children. Perhaps that's what I'll do. If so, I'll find someone like that little man on the jury, someone who'll be human and a person, like me.

  (*She suddenly cries out.*)

I've had enough. I've loved you for years and it's broken me. I'm going away and I shall never see you again. Never!

**KARL.** Lisa!

**LISA.** Never!

> (*The* **DOCTOR** *is suddenly heard calling from the hall.*)

**DOCTOR.** (*Offstage.*) Karl! Karl!

> (*He enters quite out of breath.*)

It's all right, my boy. She's acquitted. Do you understand? She's acquitted.

> (*He suddenly sees* **LISA** *and crosses to her with outstretched arms.*)

Lisa – my dear Lisa. Thank God we've got you safe. It's wonderful. Wonderful!

**LISA.** Yes, it's wonderful.

> (*The* **DOCTOR** *holds her away from him, looking her up and down.*)

**DOCTOR.** How are you? A little fine drawn – thinner – only natural with all you've been through. But we'll make it up to you. We'll look after you. As for Karl here, you can imagine the state he's been in. Ah, well, thank God that's all over now.

> (*He turns to* **KARL.**)

What do you say – shall we go out – celebrate? A bottle of champagne – eh?

> (*He beams expectantly.* **LISA** *forces a smile.*)

**LISA.** No, Doctor – not tonight.

**DOCTOR.** Ah, what an old fool I am. Of course not. You need rest.

**LISA.** I am all right. I must just get my things together.

**DOCTOR.** Things?

**LISA.** I am not – staying here.

DOCTOR. But... *(Enlightened.)* Oh, I see – well, perhaps that is wise – with people like your Mrs. Roper about, with their evil minds and tongues. But where will you go? To a hotel? Better come to us. Margaret will be delighted. It's a very tiny room that we have, but we'll look after you well.

LISA. How kind you are. But I have all my plans made. Tell – tell Margaret that I will come to see her very soon.

> *(LISA exits through the hall and into her bedroom. The DOCTOR turns back to KARL and begins to realise that all is not well.)*

DOCTOR. Karl – is anything wrong?

KARL. What should be wrong?

DOCTOR. She has been through a terrible ordeal. It takes a little time to – to come back to normal.

> *(He looks around.)*

When I think we sat here – waiting – with that damn telephone ringing all the time – hoping – fearing – and now – all over.

KARL. *(Tonelessly.)* Yes – all over.

DOCTOR. *(Robustly.)* No decent jury would ever have convicted her. I told you so. You look half dazed still, Karl. Can't you quite believe it yet?

> *(He takes KARL affectionately by the shoulders.)*

Karl, snap out of it. We've got our Lisa back again.

> *(KARL turns away.)*

Oh, I know – I'm clumsy – it takes a little time to get used to – joy.

> *(LISA enters from her bedroom carrying a hold-all. She avoids looking at KARL.)*

LISA. I'm going now.

DOCTOR. I'll get a taxi for you.

LISA. *(Sharply.)* No – please – I'd rather be alone.

> *(The DOCTOR is slightly taken aback. She relents, moves to the DOCTOR and puts her hands on his shoulders.)*

Thank you – for all your kindness – for all you did for Anya – you have been a good friend – I shall never forget.

> *(She kisses the DOCTOR. Then without once looking at KARL, she exits through the hall and out the front door.)*

DOCTOR. Karl – what does this mean? There is something wrong.

KARL. Lisa is going away.

DOCTOR. Yes, yes – temporarily. But – she is coming back.

KARL. No, she is not coming back.

DOCTOR. *(Appalled.)* What do you mean?

> *(KARL speaks with complete conviction and force.)*

KARL. She – is – not – coming – back.

DOCTOR. *(Incredulously.)* Do you mean – you have parted?

KARL. You saw her go – that was our parting.

DOCTOR. But – why?

KARL. She had had enough.

DOCTOR. Talk sense, man.

KARL. It's very simple. She has suffered. She doesn't want to suffer any more.

DOCTOR. Why should she suffer?

KARL. It seems – I am a man – who brings suffering to those who love him.

DOCTOR. Nonsense!

KARL. Is it? Anya loved me and she is dead. Helen loved me and she died.

DOCTOR. Did Lisa say that to you?

KARL. Yes. Am I such a man? Do I bring suffering to those who love me? What did she mean when she talked of fields of amaranth?

DOCTOR. Fields of amaranth.

> *(He thinks for a moment, then recollects. He picks up the copy of Walter Savage Landor and gives it to KARL.)*

Yes, I was reading there.

> *(He points to the quotation.)*

KARL. Please leave me.

DOCTOR. I'd like to stay.

KARL. I must get used to being alone.

> *(The DOCTOR hesitates.)*

DOCTOR. You don't think...?

KARL. She will not come back.

> *(The DOCTOR nods then exits, closing the doors behind him. There is a pause. KARL rises, crosses to the desk, switches on the desk light then sits and reads:.)*

"There are no fields of Amaranth this side of the grave. There are no voices, oh Rhodope, that are not soon mute, however tuneful: there is no name, with whatever emphasis of passionate love repeated, of which the echo is not faint at last..."

> *(He puts the book gently aside, rises, picks up the record, goes to the record player puts it on. He moves slowly to the armchair and sinks into it.)*

Lisa – Lisa – how can I live without you?

> *(He drops his head into his hands. There is a pause. The doors to the hall open slowly. LISA enters. She moves to KARL and puts her hand gently on his shoulder. He looks up.)*

Lisa? You've come back. Why?

*(**LISA** kneels at his side.)*

**LISA.** Because I am a fool.

*(She lovingly rests her head on **KARL**'s lap. The music builds.)*

**End of Play**

# THE AGATHA CHRISTIE COLLECTION

Agatha Christie is regarded as the most successful female playwright of all time. Her illustrious dramatic career spans forty-two years, countless acclaimed original plays, several renowned novels adapted for stage, and numerous collections of thrilling one-act plays. Testament to Christie's longevity, these plays continue to engage great artists and enthral audiences today.

Since the première of her first play in 1930 the world of theatre has changed immeasurably, and so has the way plays are published and performed. Embarking upon a two-year project, Agatha Christie Limited sought to re-open Christie's distinguished body of dramatic work, looking to both original manuscripts and the most recent publications to create a "remastered" edition of each play. Each new text would contain only the words of Agatha Christie (or adaptors she personally worked with) and all extraneous materials that might come between the interpreter and the playwright would be removed, ultimately bringing the flavor and content of the texts closer to what the author would have delivered to the rehearsal room. Each new edition would then be specifically tailored to the needs and requirements of the professional twenty-first century artist.

The result is The Collection.

Whether in a classic revival or new approach, The Collection has been purposely assembled for the contemporary theatre professional. The choice and combination of plays offers something for all tastes and kinds of performance with the skill, imagination and genius of Agatha Christie's work now waiting to be explored anew in theatre.

For more information on The Collection, please visit
agathachristielimited.com/licensing/stage/browse-by-play

Lightning Source UK Ltd.
Milton Keynes UK
UKHW010047240119
336085UK00005B/555/P